Reflections on Forgiveness and Spiritual Growth

Reflections
on
Forgiveness
and
Spiritual
Growth

Edited by
Andrew J. Weaver
and
Monica Furlong

"And forgive us our debts, as we also have forgiven our debtors."
(Matthew 6:12)

ABINGDON PRESS
Nashville

REFLECTIONS ON FORGIVENESS AND SPIRITUAL GROWTH

Library of Congress Cataloging-in-Publication Data

Reflections on forgiveness and spiritual growth / edited by Andrew J. Weaver and Monica Furlong.
    p. cm.
    Includes bibliographical references.
    ISBN 0-687-08406-7 (alk. paper)
    1. Forgiveness—Religious aspects—Christianity.   I. Weaver, Andrew J., 1947-II. Furlong, Monica.

BV4647.F55 R44 2000
234'.5—dc21   00-061840

00 01 02 03 04 05 06 07 08 09—10 9 8 7 6 5 4 3 2 1

MANUFACTURED IN THE UNITED STATES OF AMERICA

To
Carolyn
with
Aloha

So far as we can, let us always rejoice to strengthen each other's hands in God. Above all, let us each take heed unto himself (since each must give an account of himself to God) that he fall not short of the religion of love. . . . O let you and me (whatever others do) press on to the prize of our high calling—that, being justified by faith, we may have peace with God through our Lord Jesus Christ . . . that the love of God may be shed abroad in our hearts by the Holy Ghost which is given unto us.

From a letter to an Irish Roman Catholic by the Anglican priest and founder of Methodism The Rev. John Wesley, July 18, 1749

Contents

Acknowledgments

W e are thankful to the Reverend Ray Davey, O.B.E., for writing the foreword for the volume. He and his brave and dedicated colleagues in the Corrymeela Community in Northern Ireland have, since the 1960s, consistently—and at personal cost—trod the path of love through the agony of "the Troubles." A portion of the proceeds from this book goes to the Corrymeela Community for its mission of peace and justice. "Blessed are the peacemakers, for they will be called children of God" (Matthew 5:9).

We are grateful to the Reverend Carolyn L. Stapleton for her excellent editorial discernment throughout the development of this book. We are also appreciative of Ms. Christina M. DeGray for her considerable help while preparing the manuscript.

Foreword

It is chastening to consider the amount of violence and destruction in today's world. Currently the dire reality of ethnic cleansing, daily portrayed on our television screens, is only the most recent of equally frightful catalogues of mass destruction in the twentieth century, and mass destruction has been vastly escalated as modern technology ever develops more refined and deadly weapons for it.

What is the way forward for those who claim to be the followers of Christ, the Prince of Peace? Have we anything to say? What response have we to make? It is a vast and complex task because there are so many different aspects to consider depending on the way the conflict is interpreted. Is it political, religious, cultural, or social, or does it include all these aspects? All I can try to do is offer my thoughts about my own experience in a divided society here in Ireland and the things that have become real for us through our conflict.

But is there any perspective that can embrace all these factors and attempt to transcend them? I will share very briefly several responses that we in Corrymeela have tried to make through the years of "the Troubles." From the start we have tried to be a sign of hope and to incarnate it in our life together as a community. Our country is filled with signs—many of them negative and destructive. So we set out to be an inclusive community. This is how we put it at the opening of the Centre at Ballycastle in 1965: "We hope that Corrymeela will come to be known as the 'Open Village,' open to all people of goodwill who are willing to meet each other, to learn from each other, and work together for the good of all."

Through the passing years and the continuing violence in our country, we have been very conscious of our inadequacies and failures in the quest for peace. But we return again to our commitment to be "instruments of God's peace," and we are reassured again and again that we will receive the strength and the wisdom we need.

In 1985, I was invited to return to Germany where I had been a prisoner of war in 1944–45. I had been attached to Stalag IV-A as a YMCA field-worker and chaplain. My main task was to visit work camps all over the Dresden area. This was late in the war and many German cities were being attacked by Allied bombers. The climax came on 13 and 14 February 1945 when the city was devastated by three Anglo-American air raids. Thousands of incendiary bombs had ignited a massive firestorm raising the temperature to between 800 and 1000 degrees Celcius. This caused a mighty suction as the cool air rushed in to replace the rising hot air. The horrific result was that many people trying to escape from the burning city were sucked back into the inferno. No one knows how many lost their lives and estimates range from thirty thousand to one hundred thousand!

In May 1985 I was invited to go to Germany as a representative of the British Council of Churches at a gathering of representatives from the different countries that had been involved in the war. The meetings were to take place in Berlin, and I agreed to go on condition that they would arrange for me to revisit the Dresden.

That visit will always live in my memory! Our host was Cristof Ziemer who was the pastor of the ancient Kreuzkirche right in the center of the city and close to the Elbe. It was Rogation Sunday, and he invited me to take part in celebrating the eucharist and give a brief sermon. My wife, Kathleen, was asked to read the scripture. I had no time to prepare a sermon, so I just spoke from the heart. I explained how the last time I had been in their city I had been a prisoner and an enemy. I spoke very frankly about the feelings of my fellow prisoners and how much many of them had suffered with forced marches in the depth of winter. Then I went on to speak of the horrors of the raids and the sufferings and the death of so many and how saddened and shocked many of the prisoners were by what they had seen.

Finally I spoke of how, today, we were all gathered around the one Table of our Lord and here receive his forgiveness and are able to forgive each other. I concluded with Paul's words: "For Christ is our peace who has broken down the wall that separates us." I knew that I had been given those words, because I usually have to prepare what I say.

The sequel took place later at the beautiful Semper Opera House. The play was *Die Freischutz* by Carl von Weber. The last time it had been presented was forty years earlier on the night of the air raids! During the interval the lady sitting next to Kathleen began to talk to her. She explained that she had been to the service in the Kreuzkirche with her husband and how much they had been moved by what had taken place. On the night of the raid he had been in barracks, since at sixteen he was already in the army. Then she described how, in the raids, his mother, his six-year-old sister, and both his grandparents had been killed. Ever since he had been filled with hatred and bitterness against the British and the Americans and could not forgive. At this point the lights went out, and the play continued. When the program ended and the lights went up, there was a quick exodus and the husband and wife were gone. Then Kathleen told me what had happened and what the lady had said. And I replied, "I do wish I had had the chance to speak to him." However when we got out into the street, we were quickly caught up in the large crowds of people hurrying home, and I felt very disappointed that I had missed him. Then as we stood there a man came dodging between the cars and pushing his way through the people. He rushed up to me and grasped my hand. I could see that there were tears in his eyes, and he simply said, "Now I can forgive." He rung my hand again and disappeared into the crowd, and I never saw him again.

I believe that there is a rediscovery in the Christian message of forgiveness. Think of how central it is in the story of Christ. In the prayer he taught us to pray: "Forgive us . . . as we forgive." Then on the cross he prayed, "Father forgive them."

We in Corrymeela cherish our link with Coventry Cathedral through their "Cross of Nails Community." The story of the new Cathedral is a living parable of life through death: the marvelous twentieth-century building springs from the war-devastated ruins of the ancient twelfth-century building. But for me the outstanding memory is not of the modern building, but rather of the simple altar that stands within the broken walls and roofless sanctuary of the old building.

On this altar stands a fire charred wooden cross. Two beams had been rescued from the ruins, and someone had put one of the beams across and formed a cross. This had been placed on the altar and above it inscribed simply: FATHER FORGIVE. Is there any more important word for us today in Ireland or across our world?

—Ray Davey

Contributors

William J. Abraham is a United Methodist clergyperson. A graduate of Oxford University, he teaches philosophy and theology at Perkins School of Theology, Southern Methodist University, where he holds the Albert Cook Outler Chair of Wesley Studies. Dr. Abraham is the author of *Waking from Doctrinal Amnesia* (Abingdon Press) and *Canon and Criterion in Christian Theology: From the Fathers to Feminism* (Clarendon Press).

Paschal M. Baumstein, O.S.B., is a Benedictine monk at Belmont Abbey in Belmont, North Carolina, and book review editor for *Cistercian Studies Quarterly*. He has written several dozen articles for scholarly journals and two books on monastic life and history. He is on the Board of Advisors and is a contributor to the forthcoming *Encyclopedia of Monasticism*.

Roberta C. Bondi earned the Doctor of Philosophy degree at Oxford University and is Professor of Church History at Candler School of Theology, Emory University. She is author of *To Love As God Loves, To Pray and to Love, Memories of God, A Place to Pray: Reflections on the Lord's Prayer,* and *In Ordinary Time.*

Michael H. Collins is an Anglican who has received three degrees from Oxford University. He has served in various capacities in the dioceses of Sheffield and London in the United Kingdom. He is a writer and reviewer with particular interests in history, politics, and healthcare. He is currently living in Toronto, Canada.

Jim Cotter is a Cambridge graduate who pursues an ordained ministry on the fringes of the Church of England. He lives in Sheffield where he writes and publishes under Cairns Publications and whence he travels to lead retreats and speak at conferences. He has recently published two books in the United

States and Britain, *Prayer at Night's Approaching* and *Psalms for a Pilgrim People*. Both books unfold afresh some of the ancient texts of the Christian tradition.

Joseph Coyne is a graduate of the Washington Theological Union in Washington, D.C. He is a clinical psychologist who served as a priest in the Congregation of the Sacred Hearts of Jesus and Mary for twenty years. Dr. Coyne now teaches in the clinical training program at Golden Gate University in San Francisco, California.

Ray Davey, O.B.E., is a Presbyterian minister and a founder of the Corrymeela Community in Belfast, Northern Ireland, which has worked since 1965 to achieve reconciliation between the Protestants and Catholics.

Monica Furlong has worked as a journalist on Fleet Street and as a Religious Programmes Producer for the BBC. She has published many books about religion, including biographies of Thomas Merton, Alan Watts, and Therese of Lisieux. From 1982 to 1985 she was Moderator of the Movement for the Ordination of Women (advocating women's ordination in the Church of England) and wrote many articles in support of the campaign and a book describing it, *A Dangerous Delight* (1991). Her recent work includes a travel book about Aboriginal Australians in the Great Sandy Desert of Western Australia, *The Flight of the Kingfisher* (1997). At present she is authoring a study of the Church of England.

Margaret Hebblethwaite is a Catholic writer and broadcaster currently working as Assistant Editor of the *Tablet,* the international Catholic weekly. She is the author of seven books on the themes of spirituality, feminist theology, and basic ecclesial communities. Her most recent titles are *Six New Gospels: New Testament Women Tell Their Stories* (1994) and *The Way of Ignatius: Finding God in All Things* (1998). Over the years she has been involved in a number of ministries as a layperson, including prison chaplaincy work, spiritual direction, and Cathechist of Exeter College, Oxford. She is the widow of Vaticanologist Peter Hebblethwaithe.

Eric James has been Chaplain of Trinity College at Cambridge, vicar of an inner-city parish in South London, a leader of the reform and renewal movement Parish & People in the Church of England, Canon Missioner of the St. Alban's Diocese, and the director of Christian Action, a movement for social action. He persuaded Robert Runcie, then Archbishop of Canterbury, to set up a commission on urban priority areas which—among other things—made the Church of England the liveliest opposition to the conservative government during the Thatcher years. He published a distinguished biography of Bishop John A. T. Robinson and is a well-known preacher and broadcaster in Britain.

M. Basil Pennington, O.C.S.O., entered the Cistercian Order after being graduated from Cathedral College of the Immaculate Conception. After ordination he studied for several years in Rome, earning a licentiate in sacred theology and a licentiate in canon law. He assisted at the Second Vatican Council as a peritus and in the preparation of the new Code of Canon Law. With Thomas Merton he started Cistercian Publications and founded the Institute of Cistercian Studies at Western Michigan University. Father Basil is known internationally for his leadership in fostering Centering Prayer. He has published many books and articles on the spiritual life. His most recent books are *Lectio Divina: Renewing the Ancient Practice of Praying the Scriptures* (Crossroad) and *A Place Apart: Monastic Prayer and Practice for Everyone* (Ligouri). Father Basil lives at the Abbey of Our Lady of Saint Joseph, Spencer, Massachusetts.

Donald J. Shelby recently retired as senior pastor of the First United Methodist Church in Santa Monica, California, where he served for twenty-four years. He is a graduate of the School of Theology at Claremont and has authored several religious books, including *The Unsettling Season, Bold Expectations, Forever Beginning,* and *Meeting the Messiah*. He and his spouse, Jean, live in Los Osos, California.

Ronald E. Swisher is a graduate of the University of San Francisco and the Pacific School of Religion in Berkeley,

California. He has served as a district superintendent in The United Methodist Church and is an active member of Black Methodists for Church Renewal. He has served as Minister of Congregational Life at Glide Memorial United Methodist Church in San Francisco. Presently he is Senior Pastor of Taylor Memorial United Methodist Church, Oakland, California.

Barbara Brown Taylor is an Episcopal priest in the Diocese of Atlanta. She served urban and rural parishes in Georgia for fifteen years before assuming her current post as Butman Professor of Religion and Philosophy at Piedmont College in Demorest, Georgia. In recent years, she has lectured on preaching at Yale, Princeton, and Duke universities and has spoken at churches across the country. Professor Taylor is the author of eight books, including *The Luminous Web: Essays on Science and Religion* (Cowley, 2000) and *God in Pain: Teaching Sermons on Suffering* (Abingdon, 1998).

James M. Wall served from 1972 through 1999 as editor and publisher of the *Christian Century*, a publication that deals with religion and society. He is now Senior Contributing Editor, where he writes a regular column and is an advisor to the editor. Wall, a United Methodist clergyman, is also president of ForCHILDREN, a group that works with non-profit organizations in developing countries to assist them in meeting United Nations standards for children in the areas of health, education, and welfare. His most recent book is *Hidden Treasures: Searching for God in Modern Culture* (Christian Century Press).

Brendan Walsh is the head of communications for CAFOD, the Catholic Church's aid and development agency in the United Kingdom. He writes for newspapers and contributes articles to books—most recently a Lenten book, *A New Earth* (1998). He studied theology and religious studies at the universities of Lancaster and Bristol and has worked as a publisher with the Catholic Truth Society and SPCK. He lives in Limehouse in the East End of London.

Andrew J. Weaver is a United Methodist minister and licensed clinical psychologist who is codirector of research at the

HealthCare Chaplaincy in New York City. He studied theology at Ripon Hall, Oxford, and Perkins School of Theology, Southern Methodist University. Dr. Weaver has written over sixty articles and book chapters on the role of clergy in mental healthcare. He holds a doctorate in psychology and has coauthored or edited three Abingdon Press books: *Reflections on Aging and Spiritual Growth* (1998), *Counseling Troubled Older Adults: A Handbook for Pastors and Religious Caregivers* (1997), and *Counseling Troubled Teens and Their Families: A Handbook for Pastors and Youth Workers* (1999).

Halbert D. Weidner, C.O., has served as parish priest, retreat center leader, and campus minister in the United States and England. He has written articles and reviews for *Christian Century, U.S. Catholic, Liguorian, Review for Religious,* and *Catholic Digest.* Dr. Weidner has published two books, including the first Anglican work on Cardinal Newman in the Oxford University Press critical edition series of Newman's works: *The Via Media of the Anglican Church* and *Praying with John Cardinal Newman.* He is presently founding an Oratory of St. Philip Neri in his home diocese of Honolulu, Hawaii, and is pastor of Holy Trinity Church. Father Hal has a master of arts from the Graduate Theological Union in Berkeley, California, and a doctorate from Oxford University, England. He was a Dillistone Scholar at Oriel College, Oxford.

William H. Willimon is Dean of the Chapel and Professor of Christian Ministry at Duke University in Durham, North Carolina. He directs the programs of campus ministry at Duke and teaches in the divinity and undergraduate schools. Dr. Willimon has given lectures at colleges and universities throughout the United States, Europe, and Asia. He is the author of more than forty books. His most recent book is *The Last Word*, published by Abingdon Press. Dr. Willimon has earned degrees from Wofford College, Yale University, and Emory University. Six colleges and universities have awarded him honorary degrees.

Introduction:
Forgiveness and Faith—
What Does Science Say?

Andrew J. Weaver

T o err is human, to forgive divine," wrote the eighteenth-century English poet Alexander Pope. Interestingly, scientific studies have found that people often link their ability to forgive with their faith. In a national survey of Americans, more than eight out of ten (83 percent) reported that God's help was needed to be able to truly forgive another person, while only 15 percent indicated that they could forgive using their own power and resources. An active prayer life, feeling close to God, and the importance of faith were associated with forgiving. Furthermore, people who tend to be forgiving report more satisfaction in life.[1] Nine American adults in ten say they pray, and nearly all who pray ask forgiveness for themselves and others.[2]

On the other hand, researchers have found that seeking revenge can be bad for your mental health. People who dwell on fantasies of revenge against others tend to report greater psychological distress.[3] To the extent that forgiveness helps reduce a desire for revenge, forgiveness may assist people in avoiding mental health difficulties. In a study of elderly women in the midwestern United States, the capacity for forgiveness was associated with self-esteem and good mental health.[4]

Faith and forgiveness have been found to be important factors in successful marriages. Couples report that faith facilitates decision making, minimizes conflicts, increases tolerance,[5] fosters marital commitment, and is associated with long-term marriage.[6] The ability to forgive is also an important element in marital success. Couples who had been married for more than twenty years indicated that the capacity to seek and grant forgiveness is essential to marital longevity and satisfaction.[7]

Some mental health specialists are advocating for the inclusion of forgiveness as a part of several modes of therapy. In a survey of 101 therapists in North Carolina, most saw forgiveness as useful in some treatments, especially with family- and marital-relationship problems and reactions to loss.[8] The therapists also noted that the timing of forgiveness is important. For example, individuals who are in abusive relationships need their anger to set limits with the abuser. Premature forgiveness can be a cover for passivity, avoidance, and fear. Forgiveness is a long-term process when the wound is deep, and no one should be coerced into forgiving.

Faith is often used by people who have been victimized and are faced with painful psychological wounds that need healing. In addition to offering the social support of community, nurturing religion provides a healing means of addressing a traumatic experience. Faith can enhance well-being, lower distress, and may facilitate faster and more effective emotional recovery.[9] In a study of more than twelve hundred men, those who had suffered physical or sexual child abuse were more likely to use prayer and other spiritual resources to cope than those not victimized.[10] In fact, the more severe the abuse, the greater the use of faith resources in their life.

Researchers Radhi Al-Mabuk and William Downs[11] have used the process of forgiveness as a part of their therapy with parents who suffer the traumatic loss of a child by suicide. Such parents have a mixture of intense and contradictory emotions. Their grief over the death can be complicated by anger at the child, along with intense self-blame, shame, and guilt for failing to prevent the suicide. Parents often live the traumatic event over and over, unable to emotionally move on with their lives. In forgiveness therapy, the parents are helped to face their pain, release their rage, and develop empathy for the suffering of their child. The scientists found that the process of seeking self-forgiveness and giving forgiveness to the child helped the relatives to reduce anger, guilt, anxiety, and depression, as well as increasing self-esteem and hope. Since suicide is the second leading cause of death among children and youth in the United States[12] there is a critical need to find ways to help the loved ones recover from this psychological trauma.

These and other research findings have led the John Templeton Foundation to fund a five-million-dollar research project on forgiveness. The foundation has enlisted luminaries such as former U.S. President Jimmy Carter and the Nobel Laureate Archbishop Desmond Tutu to help raise an additional five million dollars for forgiveness research in places like Northern Ireland and South Africa.

Reflections on Forgiveness and Spiritual Growth gives creative and profound voices from within the Roman Catholic, Anglican, and Protestant communities an opportunity to reflect on forgiveness as a part of their faith journey and share with us their insights. What counsel does our Christian heritage offer us as we give, seek, or receive forgiveness? What lessons and wisdom can be shared about our personal struggle to forgive or be forgiven? Does forgiveness mean we forget? Does forgiveness end resentment? Are there some things that are unforgivable? What is the relationship between forgiving, seeking justice, and reconciling? Can prayer help us forgive? Does forgiving lead to deeper faith? What spiritual direction might be offered to others on the journey of faith who are struggling with forgiveness?

It is our hope that the wisdom in this book can help us to understand and appreciate more fully Jesus' simple commandment to "forgive as we have been forgiven." Science is beginning to confirm that as we learn to seek and grant forgiveness, we and our families will become emotionally (and, one hopes, spiritually) healthier.

Notes

1. Poloma, M. M. & Gallup, G. H. (1991). Unless You Forgive Others: Prayer and Forgiveness. In *Varieties of Prayer* (pp. 85-106). Philadelphia: Trinity Press.

2. Gallup, G. H. (1996). *Religion in America: 1996*. Princeton, NJ: The Gallup Organization.

3. Greenwald, D. F. & Harder, D. W. (1994). Sustaining Fantasies and Psychopathology in a Normal Sample. *Journal of Clinical Psychology, 50*(5), 707-710.

4. Hebl, J. H. & Enright, R. D. (1993). Forgiveness As a Psychotherapeutic Goal with Elderly Females. *Psychotherapy, 30*, 658-667.

5. Robinson, L. C. (1994). Religious Orientation in Enduring Marriage: An Exploratory Study. *Review of Religious Research, 35,* 207-218.

6. Robinson, L. C. & Blanton, P. W. (1993). Marital Strengths in Enduring Marriages. *Family Relations, 42,* 38-45.

7. Fenell, D. (1993). Characteristics of Long-term First Marriages. *Journal of Mental Health Counseling, 15*(4), 446-460.

8. Denton, R. T. & Martin, M. W. (1998). Defining Forgiveness: An Empirical Exploration of Process and Role. *American Journal of Family Therapy, 26,* 281-292.

9. Pargament, K. I. (1997). *The Psychology of Religion and Coping: Theory, Research, Practice.* New York: Guilford Press.

10. Lawson, R., Drebing, C., Berg, G., Vincellette, A., & Penk, W. (1998). The Long Term Impact of Child Abuse on Religious Behavior and Spirituality in Men. *Child Abuse and Neglect, 22*(5), 369-380.

11. Al-Mabuk, R. & Downs, W. (1996). Forgiveness Therapy with Parents of Adolescent Suicide Victims. *Journal of Family Psychotherapy, 7*(2), 21-39.

12. Weaver, A. J., Preston, J. D., & Jerome, L. W. (1999). *Counseling Troubled Teens and Their Families: A Handbook for Pastors and Youth Workers.* Nashville: Abingdon Press.

Forgiveness, Judgmentalism, and the Sense of Self

Roberta C. Bondi

H ow many times must I forgive my brother?" Peter asked Jesus one day, under what he was experiencing, presumably, as extreme provocation, "as many as seven times?"

"Only seven times?" Jesus answered him. "You've got to be joking; seven times is hardly even a start!"

"Teach us to pray as John the Baptist taught his disciples," the apostles asked Jesus on another occasion. He replied, "Of course," and he taught them the Lord's Prayer—including the line "forgive us our trespasses as we forgive those who trespass against us."

The implications of these words of Jesus must have been clear to his early listeners: do not ask God for forgiveness for the injuries you do to others and God unless you are prepared first to forgive those who injure you. Were Jesus' disciples sorry they had asked Jesus for this prayer? I imagine some of them must surely have been. There have been innumerable times when I have been sorry myself. There is no getting around the fact that Jesus does not seem to leave us much elbow room in the matter of forgiveness. I still remember with excruciating clarity reading the parable of the unforgiving servant (Matthew 18:23-35) in Sunday school as an early adolescent, then coming home afterward to look with a mixture of rage and anxiety at my two deliberately tormenting younger brothers. The parable seemed to me to be perfectly straightforward. If I could not forgive them for their relentless teasing, it would be all over for me. In a flash, in the very moment of my death, I could count on finding myself cast into outer darkness to the place where there would be wailing and gnashing of teeth.

27

Forgiveness is not always difficult, of course, even for the most stony-hearted of us. We can be "trespassed against" every day and still find it easy to forgive "those who trespass against us." Sometimes we might think that it is because these offenses are trivial or that we are just naturally forgiving people: our spouses forget what they were to pick up for us at the store or the normally considerate neighbor runs over our garbage can backing out of the driveway. The injuries we find easy to forgive are not always trivial, however. Serious damage can be done to us: a doctor may make a significant error in judgment with respect to the treatment of an illness. We may be very sorry about having to live or even die with the consequences of the doctor's error, but because we have always found her to be habitually conscientious and committed to the well-being of her patients in the past, we are still able to say, and mean it from the bottom of our hearts, "Of course, I forgive her; all of us make mistakes."

At one time or another, however, forgiveness seems to be almost impossible for most of us who would walk in Jesus' path. This is because sooner or later we are each confronted by another kind of injury that appears to strike at the very core of who we think we are. We respond to the infliction of these hurts as though our very selves have been wounded or even taken away.

I have a friend a few years younger than I, whose parents were divorced when she was five. Her father, a college professor, has never paid any attention to her since. Though he has expected her to acknowledge all of his special occasions, he has regarded all her birthdays, Christmases, and graduations as being of little consequence in comparison to his need to grade papers or prepare lectures. It is hardly surprising that she has had to spend a great deal of her adult life trying both to come to a sense of herself as a valuable person and to forgive her father. Having been or being on the receiving end of child or spouse abuse or systematic racism, receiving harsh treatment due to a disability, being treated as an apparent nonentity at work or at home—all of these are examples of the major hard-to-forgive wounds to our sense of self that I am talking about.

Obviously big wounds to our sense of self, however, are not the only ones that can frustrate our attempts to forgive.

Surprisingly, apparently trivial offenses can seem to wound us equally in our sense of self. For example, a small slight from a friend, rudeness from a clerk in a store or from another driver on the road, or an inconsiderate phone call late at night can lay us low in the matter of forgiveness. Generally, I suspect this is because these apparent small injuries somehow put us back in the place of earlier injuries to our sense of self. This was the case, I know, with my friend's rejection by her father. A careless word from a clerk in a store can sometimes feel to her like a confirmation of the rightness of her father's rejection. To some degree, all of us suffer some variation of this theme.

So what are we to do with this second type of injury that we react to as though our very being is threatened? For me, my starting place is in the recognition that I am somehow colluding in my own injury by secretly believing, like many of us raised as Christians, that if I were a really good person, I would not mind my injuries because my hurts only come from wanting to *have* a self in the first place. Did Jesus not say, after all, that if folks wanted to be good people and follow him, then they must take up their cross, lose their lives in order to find them, and turn the other cheek when they are struck? During the time when I grew up, these verses were thought to apply especially to married women and mothers, who were expected not just to sacrifice for the people they loved, but to sacrifice their actual selves. "Oh, she is such a good Christian woman; she is just selfless," I heard again and again of a woman I knew who had given up her own hopes and desires in exchange for her husband's career; whose husband, children, and sometimes, parents took the things she did for them as their natural right; a woman who was in church working every time the doors were open; a woman who did all of these things without any recognition except for her "selflessness."

Of course, I admired this woman and her fortitude in her attempt to completely give herself over, as she would have said, to the works of love. Nonetheless, once I got very far past my own adolescence, I, being an observant person, quickly began to learn something about myself: that any attempt on my part to be truly "selfless"—that is, to give myself away—quickly produced the very opposite of what I was striving for as a Christian, which was growth in my ability to love God and neighbor. Observation told me I was not the only person with this problem, either. There were many women like me, and men, too, who had been raised on this same myth. I still meet many of them in the classes I teach in seminary.

How many of us, having misunderstood what Jesus is really calling us to, have had to suffer the bone-crushing depression that can come in the wake of a longtime attempt to be selfless in this manner? How many struggle in vain against being over-sensitive or a simmering resentment toward those we imagine are putting us in a position where we must give up our own needs and desires to cater to theirs? How can they expect this sacrifice without feeling any need to reciprocate? It can be hard not to act out our depression through criticism of those around us or through general judgmentalism toward those we believe are getting away with something we think we have to do to be good people!

I particularly hate what I see when those who feel called to ordained ministry suffer from this split, believing that they should be selfless and knowing what happens when they actually try to be selfless. It does not seem to take them long to burn out through unnecessary overwork or to become resentful, self-righteous pastors whose refusal to claim time for rest, study, or even prayer makes the lives of their families, as well as their parishioners, miserable.

But if part of us does not believe we ought to have selves of our own in the first place, how does all of this relate to our ability to forgive wounds to what we perceive to be those selves? It means, for one thing, that if we tell ourselves the truth, we have to admit that very often we do not even *want* to forgive. This is not because we are nasty, ungenerous people. Rather, it is because God gives us the knowledge through the grace of experience that forgiveness is going to be harmful to us if we believe it means that we must say to our injurers, "It is all right that you have attacked my self; I shouldn't have one, anyway. I still love you no matter what you do; go ahead and do with me as it pleases you."

It is important to be clear, however, that whatever we have been reared to believe, this is not what Jesus means by forgiveness. As I understand Jesus' teaching in the Gospels, Jesus never tells anyone to turn his or her very soul over to someone else, or even to like that person, after that person is forgiven. Rather, forgiveness has only two, admittedly difficult, requirements: (1) that we give up the idea of revenge against our injurers, of holding them accountable for every bit of the "debt" they owe us (we are to let go of the old law of "an eye for an eye") and (2) that we pray for the well-being of those who spitefully use us.

It is also important to be clear that when Jesus asks folks in the Gospels to lose their lives in order to save them or to take up their crosses to follow him, he is not talking about giving up their God-given selves to other people as though those selves are worth nothing. I think what Jesus is asking them (us) instead is to distinguish between that which *really* makes them (us) who they (we) are from those things that only seem to give them (us) value as people. It is only the image of this "false self," as some traditions call it, that Jesus asks us to give up—the self constructed out of our position in life, our families, our work, our possessions, our desires and fantasies, and other people's desires, fantasies, and approval or disapproval.

In the Gospels these selves are constructed of the same things our modern socially constructed selves are made from. In Jesus' parable of the man who built barns (Luke 12:16-21), for example, it was the things he owned, his surplus grain and the barns he would build in which to keep it. In other parables and sayings by Jesus, false images of the self are built out of admirable accomplishments, even legitimate religious accomplishments. We see this in the story of the rich young ruler (Luke 18:18-30) who could not give up his wealth, his social position, or his very real acts of goodness in order to follow Jesus. The same point is made in the parable of the Pharisee and the publican (Luke 18:9-14), and we find it as well in Jesus' radical statement that the person who would come after him must abandon his own father's funeral to do so.

Does Jesus not expect us to care about other people at all? If we look at Jesus we know this just cannot be the fact. We are social creatures who are constructed by God in such a way that we take a major portion of our identity from our human relationships and our place in the society in which we live. Surely, if Jesus really had meant for us to live in isolation, indifferent to the people with whom we share our world, he never would have asked us to love God and our neighbor as ourselves (a commandment which implies in its very wording that we are to love ourselves as well as others).

The trouble comes not with our being social creatures, but with the conviction most of us have that deep down we have no other identity—much less a primary identity—outside of what we do, what we own, or how much other people value us. How many mothers do we know who cannot evaluate their very being without considering whether they are, or at least appear to be, "good mothers" to their children? How many school-aged children value themselves only according to their popularity at school? How many ministers judge—and are encouraged by the hierarchies of their denominations to judge—the value of their ministry and so themselves by the "success" of their churches, which are measured only by size and the salary they pay? No wonder we are so reluctant to let go of an injury if we think we are being asked by Jesus, for the sake of forgiveness, to give up all that we believe there is to us of value. No wonder even a slight can feel like a mortal wound!

Nevertheless, no matter how much we may believe that other human beings have the power to take away our most fundamental selves simply by their judgments on us or their claiming a right to judge us, this is not true.[1] The fact is we cannot lose our most basic selves as people of infinite worth or have it taken away from us, either. This is because our inmost identity, even when we are unaware that it exists, comes to us from God by virtue of the fact that it is God who made us and God who loves us and has always loved us, in spite of what we or any other human being considers to be our worthiness or unworthiness. Indeed, it is because our true selves belong to God that we get into so much trouble when we try to give ourselves away to others. We cannot be selfless because, strictly speaking, our selves do not belong to us in the first place.

It is when a person really begins to believe that what I have just said is true (and it is certainly faithful to the gospel, which assures us of God's steadfast love and care for us), that that person can also begin to be able to afford to forgive those injuries that wound our sense of self. We start to be able to forgive, not so much because we no longer believe that we have been injured—in many cases we have—but because we really are learning through experience that we are not about to cease to exist if we lose our possessions, experience failure, find our bodies attacked, or suffer the disapproval of others.

It is all very well, however, to say that because our fundamental identity lies in God, we can afford to forgive those injuries that feel so threatening to our very being. None of us can come to believe this simply by gritting our teeth and willing ourselves to do it; it is much harder and takes much longer than that. At the same time, it is something I believe we can come to with patience. The ancient Christian teachers of the fourth and fifth century have given me some hints that I have found extremely helpful in my own traveling along the path to forgiveness. Let me pass along three of these hints to you.

First, I find it useful to ponder regularly, with my intellect and my heart, the implications of a line written by the fifth-century North African Christian Augustine of Hippo. At the beginning of his great spiritual autobiography and prayer, Augustine tells God (and through God, us his readers) that because God made human beings for God's self, human hearts can find no peace until they rest in, and so come to be themselves in, the God for whom they were made. Here, Augustine reminds me that my problem is not just a matter of trying to hang on to the socially constructed self I have: he is telling me that I can never find ultimate satisfaction either in clinging to this self or in giving it away to others. This is not because I am a sinner or because there is something inherently wrong with work or accomplishments or family or possessions, but because it is not the way I, as a human being, am made. I am made this way instead: as a human being, it is only as I begin to long for the loving, ever-generous God who longs for me, that I begin to find a mysterious and welcoming home in God. In that place I can look in the mirror, recognize my own face not only as good but as infinitely lovable to God, and thus truly know that my self is unlosable.

Second, as for how we can arrive at this knowledge, I am afraid it is not simply by thinking it through. Most of us are much better at talking about what we do or do not believe about

33

God and ourselves than at encountering God and being encountered by the God who created and loves us. The ancient teachers with whom I try to share my life, on the other hand, were convinced that we only learn who God is by trying to share a life with God. Thus, from them I have learned the usefulness of making a commitment to the sort of discipline of daily prayer that enables me to meet—and be met—on a regular, everyday, mundane basis by this God. Abba Arsenius used to say that "if we seek God, [God] will show [Godself] to us, and if we keep [God], [God] will remain close to us," and I have found this to be true.

With respect to the question of what type of prayer is most helpful,[2] I would suggest making use of the psalms and Gospels, particularly, but also use the kind of prayer that involves simply sitting in silence in God's presence for a time each day without any expectation of yourself or God, just as you might sit comfortably with an intimate friend or spouse without conversation.[3]

Finally, I have been taught the importance of understanding and believing that we make progress in the Christian life slowly, whether in the matter of finding our primary selves in God or in being able to forgive. A monk in the Egyptian desert once told his teacher that he had gotten so far behind in his prayers that he could not get himself to begin again. His teacher replied in this way:

> A man had a plot of land. And through his carelessness brambles sprang up and it became a wilderness of thistles and thorns. Then he decided to cultivate it. So he said to his son: "Go and clear that land." So the son went to clear it, and saw that the thistles and thorns had multiplied. . . . He said: "How much time shall I need to clear and weed all this?" And he lay on the ground and went to sleep. He did this day after day.
>
> When his father finally came to check on his progress, his son told him why he had done nothing.
>
> "Son [his father answered], if you had cleared each day the area on which you lay down, your work would have advanced slowly and you would not have lost heart." So the lad did what his father said, and in a short time the plot was cultivated.

With this story the ancient teachers remind me, and you, too, I hope, that we are most apt to become demoralized and give up altogether when we expect that we ought to get whatever we are attempting to do on the first try rather than realizing that healing the patterns of seeing, feeling, thinking, and acting that debilitate us in the Christian life is a slow process. We go forward, lose ground, stand still for a while, then go forward again. The amount of time that is involved in this process is not bad news, however, but good: after all, learning to love, including learning to forgive, is our life's work as Christians.

Notes

1. Let me be careful how I word this here, however; I do not in any way want to minimize or dismiss the suffering of people who have experienced or witnessed atrocities such as the torture and murder of their children before their eyes, or endured pain so literally unendurable that they did not think they could bear it. I realize they have had very good reason to feel like they have lost an irreplaceable part of themselves.

2. The first two chapters of my book *In Ordinary Time: Healing the Wounds of the Heart* (Abingdon Press, 1995) are designed to help the reader with issues about setting up a discipline of prayer. See also *To Pray and to Love: Conversations with the Early Church* (Fortress Press, 1991).

3. Evagrius Ponticus, who first taught this form of prayer in the fourth century, called it "pure" prayer. Many modern people know it is as "centering" prayer or "breath" prayer. Contrary to popular belief, this type of prayer is not the invention of Buddhism but has significant roots in the ancient church.

Take the First Step: Forgive Yourself

James M. Wall

E ver notice that once you start thinking seriously about something, it becomes the prism through which you begin to view everything? Take forgiveness, for example. I started thinking seriously about the concept of forgiveness and first thing I knew, every conversation I held, every book I read, and every movie I saw emerged with something to say about forgiveness—some things that were positive, others that were negative.

Through this prism I discovered many examples of the impossibility of forgiveness in serious things, and a few examples of how easy and inexpensive it is to forgive the little stuff. A spouse forgets to put the cap back on the toothpaste, and a forgiving mate just chuckles and sees the slip as endearing (of course, if there is tension in the marriage, the missing cap is seen as an example of overall thoughtlessness and may soon serve as a provocation for a major marital row, but that's another story for another time).

I also discovered that forgiveness is not just an intellectual concept; it is an intimate connection which touches us, or fails to touch us, at some mysterious part of our inner existence. We are talking here about an awareness that resonates with our entire being, and this makes describing the giving and receiving of forgiveness a difficult task. How do you really know that you have forgiven or feel forgiven? The answer is not unlike the answer to the question, how do you know you are loved: by God, by others, by yourself? I believe you know when you are able to testify, as the man who met Jesus did, "One thing I know, that though I was blind, now I see."

One way I have found to convey this mysterious process of forgiveness is to point to works of cinematic and literary art in which an author has sharply defined a situation in which forgiveness is experienced. Creative works possess a laser-beam capacity to isolate all else in the experience; the writer or the filmmaker brings to the description of this intimate moment of forgiveness a honed-down version of reality, one that is unencumbered by the complex ambiguity of years of personal experience and memories. Ambiguity is present, of course, because art, at its best, tells its story at a complex and ambiguous level. But these works of fiction enable the author to create a story, and an experience, that is effective as an enhancer of our understanding because the story is not encumbered with the baggage that comes with real-life experiences.

Personal, real-life testimonies come to us as powerful statements of forgiveness, but it is difficult to hear such testimonies without the realization that we are not hearing the entire story; we hear only the biased testimony of the storyteller. The fictional work, on the other hand, is entirely within the hands of the creative artist who presents his or her vision in such a manner that we experience the power of a moment of forgiveness, or a failure to find forgiveness, in a view as near to godlike as we are able to obtain within human thought.

The artist also has the advantage of being able to indulge in extremes. The more serious the breach in a relationship, the more difficult it is to forgive. Start with something as unforgivable, for example, as child abuse. Few experiences can strike one at the very center of his or her being as this incredibly evil act that deprives a person of so many things, including innocence, the ability to love others, and the loss of any sense of safety within the family circle.

Child abuse is of such a horrendous nature that we find ourselves saying, "Only God can forgive such behavior." Precisely. I firmly believe that one reason I trust in the existence of a loving, caring, creator God is that only such a God can address the various forms of unpardonable evil that we encounter in our lives. Human forgiveness and human love are flawed because they are never absolute. But God's love for creation and its creatures is absolute—an absoluteness that is demonstrated, and therefore revealed totally, in the sacrifice of God's son on the cross.

It is our responsibility to forgive others, even as we have been forgiven by God; and in the same manner, it is because we have been forgiven by God that we have the capacity to accept and forgive others. Since forgiving others is such an incredibly difficult step, especially of those violations which are so damaging to trust in a relationship, it becomes imperative that we begin the process of forgiving others by first forgiving ourselves. And this cannot be done alone. God's grace is required to break through the barrier we establish to prevent anyone from viewing the depth of our own refusal to forgive ourselves.

Just how deep is this refusal? Recently, while reading Henry James's novel *The Wings of a Dove,* I came across an unfamiliar word which sums up nicely the "location" of our deep-seated hidden refusal to forgive ourselves. It is to this deep level that God must go to jerk us out of our denial. Writes James, in reference to the deceitfulness of one of his characters, a man who has wasted his life in debauchery,

> She was glad to be spared the sight of such *penetralia* [emphasis added] but it would have reminded her a little less that there was no truth in him. This was the weariness of every fresh meeting; he dealt out lies as he might the cards from the greasy old pack for the game of diplomacy to which you were to sit down with him.[1]

The word *penetralia* is seldom used today, but a dictionary definition indicates that it refers to the innermost part of one's physical existence or the deepest, innermost part of a place, such as a temple or palace. It is a word that could also refer to the most hidden parts of a person's nature; and it is to these "parts" that God speaks about our inability to forgive ourselves. It is here that God lays claim upon us and says, "You are forgiven, now go and forgive others."

Not to forgive others is to consign ourselves to a life of either deep emotional pain or a state of lifelessness in which we use considerable energy denying that pain. In the movie *One Thousand Acres,* based on Jane Smiley's novel of that name (which itself is loosely based on Shakespeare's *King Lear*), two sisters suffer the pain of lifelong resentment against a father who has molested them as children and teenagers (an obvious departure from Shakespeare's narrative). There is no reconciliation in the story; the sisters continue to feel anger toward the man who robbed them of their innocence and deprived them of a natural progression from childhood to adulthood. One sister dies of cancer and on her deathbed laments to her sister how much she feels her life has been a series of failures. To the reader or the viewer, it is clear that her failures are not in what she did or did not do with her life but in her refusal to come to terms with the central evil done to her by her father. She could not forgive him.

In a 1965 movie, *Mickey One*, written by Alan Surgal, directed by Arthur Penn, and starring Warren Beatty, Mickey, a young stand-up comedian and musician, is running away from some vague threat to his life. He says to his girlfriend, "All I know is I'm guilty." Asked what he is guilty of, he responds, "Guilty of not being innocent." I talked with Alan Surgal more than thirty years after he wrote the script for *Mickey One* and asked him what the source of the obvious religious sensibility behind the picture was. He told me that at the time the film was made he had been reading sermons by theologian Paul Tillich, and he was impressed with Tillich's observation that, as Surgal put it, "the only answer to absolute hopelessness is absolute hope."

Indeed, *Mickey One*, Surgal says, is essentially a film that tells the story of a man who finally decides he will stop running from the unknown fears in his life. He chooses to have "the courage to be"—the title, by the way, of one of Tillich's books. When Mickey stops running and confronts his fears, he does so because he finds the courage to be, an act in which his guilt falls away and releases him into a hopeful future. (The film also contains several references to Jeremiah's question, "Is there any word from the Lord?"—a question Surgal picked up from one of Tillich's sermons.)

I began this discussion by setting forth one of the worst violations of the human experience—child abuse—because the best way to think of the difficulty of forgiveness is to begin at the extremes. But from that outer limit of behavior, we do not

40

have to travel far into the behavioral scale to find ourselves, our actions, and our attitudes crying out for forgiveness. It is for this reason that any discussion of forgiveness must begin with our willingness to accept God's forgiveness of ourselves and, consequently, our willingness to forgive ourselves.

Movies, at their artistic best, offer insights about forgiveness at this point of acceptance, even though secular movies rarely address the issue of God as the sole entity with the capacity to forgive our misdeeds. What I have found in viewing many films over the years is that filmmakers who themselves may not be "believers" in an ultimate being are nevertheless, as artists, aware that the act of forgiving makes no sense unless there is a transcendent realm (something other than the human dimension) that the artist can evoke. Without that which is more than the merely human, all that is left is the balancing of good and evil in human existence, and that scale is always going to tilt in the direction of wrongdoing, because self-centeredness defines the human condition.

Saving Private Ryan has emerged as a film of the late 1990s that will, no doubt, set the standard for future films depicting war as a destructive arena in which random deaths and the brutality of war are seen in frightening detail. It is also a film that contains a significant moment showing the need for forgiveness in a situation that demands our serious attention.

Director Stephen Spielberg tells the story of a small group of American soldiers, led by Captain John Miller (Tom Hanks), who, a few days after D day, are assigned the task of finding Private James Francis Ryan somewhere along the front in France. Ryan is the fourth child in a family of four sons; his three brothers have all been killed in action. The army wants to save the last remaining son so that his mother will not receive a fourth telegram.

Captain Miller's squad, which has survived the initial attack on Omaha Beach, grumbles about the assignment as an act of "public relations," but Miller, a high school teacher in civilian life, tells his men they have their orders. They proceed, plunging deeper into the chaos of the front lines, and at one point following the deaths of two members of their squad, Private Reiben (Edward Burns) threatens to walk away from the

41

assignment. He stays, however, and when they locate Ryan (Matt Damon) and are caught up in a battle in a French village, Ryan and Reiben line up behind some rubble to await the enemy.

Reiben has been angrily seething at the cost in the lives of his two buddies and the potential loss of his own life because of what he sees as a public relations gesture. He stares at Ryan, the cause of all his current misery; Ryan turns to look at him. Nothing is said. But Reiben nods slightly, a clear indication that what is past is past; together they will now face an uncertain future together. This is a scene of reconciliation, initiated by Reiben, who forgives Ryan for being the source of Reiben's own personal suffering. And Ryan, who did not ask to be rescued and so does not feel any of this is truly his "responsibility," acknowledges the nod. In that small moment, the two young men are forgiving each other.

I watched a television discussion of this film by several historians who presumed that a film could not depict subtle emotional feelings except through action or dialogue. This is a misunderstanding of the power of film as an art form. It is through context and circumstances, as well as facial expressions, body language, editing, lighting, and camera direction, that a director can evoke the "interiority" of a character, conveying, as in this instance, an act of forgiveness. (This is, of course, the problem with art; you either "see" the vision of the artist or you do not. Many viewers of works of art, like listeners of music who are tone deaf, cannot see and thereby miss what is placed before them.)

In a scene following this quiet exchange between Reiben and Ryan, a soldier loses his nerve and fails to come to the rescue of a buddy who is killed in hand-to-hand combat. Later this soldier shoots the German soldier who has killed his buddy, but he knows there is nothing he can ever do that will atone for his failure to come to his friend's rescue. He has "failed" in a combat situation—a failure many viewers will immediately identify with, not just those who have been in combat, but all of us who know that in any given situation, we have not done our best and must now live with the consequences; a burden that, to one degree or another, is basic to the human condition. Only God can offer a full pardon for this inevitable guilt found at the heart of the human condition.

And what about Private Ryan, whose own life was saved at the cost of the lives of others? We need not have been in combat to recognize that this particular burden is common to the human situation. Everyone's life experiences include those we have benefited from at a cost to others, either through a sacrifice, personal suffering, or both. In having to live with this realization, we discover that we do not deserve the gifts that come to us—certainly not when measured on a balanced scale. All that we have in this life is a gift of grace, unmerited and unearned.

Saving Private Ryan ends on a note that goes against this understanding of unmerited and unearned grace—a depiction that would not have been pleasing to Paul Tillich, who reminded us that the courage to be is the courage to accept the gift of the grace of God in spite of our inability to earn or deserve that grace. Ryan is told that now that he has been saved at such a cost, the rest of his life he must "earn" what has been given him. As an old man, grieving over his fallen comrades, Ryan begs his wife to reassure him that he has been a good man and has led a good life. His life has been saved, but he carries into old age the burden of not having earned that gift, and he cannot, therefore, pay his debt for the gift presented to him. In the film's flawed conclusion, Ryan continues to seek reassurance that the life he has led is balanced with the lives sacrificed in the mission to save him. Ryan cannot forgive himself for not having done enough to justify what has been done for him; Spielberg concludes his picture in a mood of despair that is not mitigated by the waving of the U.S. flag, the same image with which the film opens. Patriotism is no substitute for the peace of mind that comes from the assurance that balancing the scale of behavior is not humanly possible. What is possible is that God's gift of grace eliminates any need to balance the scales between what we have done and what we have failed to do.

Movies do not have to overtly refer to God to offer the forgiveness that can come only from a realm other than the human. Movies can, however, tell a story of forgiveness that finds a resolution through experiences that rise above mere human exchanges. This is the case with *Smoke Signals*, which is one of the first major American films written, directed, and performed by Native Americans that portrays the Native American experience. It is a quiet, understated portrait of a young man, Arnold Joseph, who is embittered against his father who deserted him years ago, and who must now travel from Idaho to Arizona to pick up all that his dead father left behind: his truck and his ashes.

Joseph travels to Arizona with a childhood companion, Thomas Builds-the-Fire, who possesses a spiritual serenity that permits him to accept his own limitations and emboldens him to confront Joseph with the emotional damage Joseph's anger against his father causes him. *Smoke Signals* is a "road movie." It involves an actual journey that culminates in a resolution through which the central characters achieve a degree of understanding of both themselves and one another (or, as in some road movies, they fail to reach such an understanding; *Easy Rider* is one major example of this genre).

When he reaches Arizona, Joseph meets Suzy Song, the young woman who lived with the father during his final years. Suzy helps Joseph to see his father from her perspective, as a man in grief over leaving his family and carrying the dark secret of a personal failure earlier in life. By understanding his father from Suzy's perspective, Joseph is free to begin to accept his father's failures and, finally, to forgive him. Forgiveness in this instance is a process where others cast a new light onto our bitterness and reveal for us a reason to forgive that we could not have reached alone.

It may not be the filmmaker's intention, at least not consciously, but the case can be made that something (the believer will not hesitate to infer God) works to move Joseph out of his preoccupation with his own anger and into an ability to finally forgive his father. The experience changes him dramatically; his bitterness gives way to an openness to others, including an openness to his friend Thomas, a character the viewer has already discovered to be a sensitive, humorous, caring companion.

The parable of the prodigal son (Luke 15:11-32) offers a story of forgiveness which defies logic and reason. As the elder brother correctly points out, it is neither just nor fair that his younger brother should be rewarded with the fatted calf and the father's outpouring of love, while the elder brother receives no such reward for having remained steadfast in the employ of the father. The prodigal son has squandered his inheritance and, by any human standard, should have to pay dearly for his misdeeds, including eating whatever leftover food could be found in the hog trough. But God's forgiveness is not measured by human standards, as Jesus points out in telling this parable to his followers.

The prodigal son was contrite, which is to say, he knew he had done wrong and was prepared to pay the penalty in order to earn back his father's love, but it was the contrition, not the penalty, that his father sought. All the father would ask of his son was that he return home. By human standards of justice, the lavish treatment of the repentant brother is not the fair way to deal with the two brothers. It is, in fact, grossly unfair to the elder brother, who has stayed at home and done his duty while his brother squandered his share of his father's inheritance gift. But God's forgiveness transcends human logic.

Rembrandt, in his marvelous painting *The Return of the Prodigal Son,* captures simultaneously the stern disapproval of the older brother, the joy of the father, and the contrition and gratitude of the prodigal son. The painting shows the forgiving father leaning over his returning son, both of the father's hands placed gently on the boy's shoulders. The boy wears ragged clothing, his left foot is bare, and a sandal lying nearby. The light in the painting highlights the father and son, but the elder brother stands to the right, his face gazing down with a look that does not conceal his quite human puzzlement that, despite his loyalty and steadfastness, the prodigal, who has done nothing to earn his father's love, is, before his eyes, being embraced by a forgiving parent.

Henri Nouwen wrote a detailed study of this painting in *The Return of the Prodigal Son: A Meditation on Fathers, Brothers, and Sons.* He describes this moment: "All my attention was drawn to the hands of the old father pressing his returning boy to his chest. I saw forgiveness, reconciliation, healing; I also saw safety, rest, being at home."[2]

Elsewhere in his study of the painting, Nouwen reminds us

that the one who is forgiven must now assume the task of forgiving others. Nouwen believes one of Jesus' sayings is "perhaps the most radical statement ever made: 'Be compassionate as your Father is compassionate.' God's compassion is described by Jesus not simply to show me how willing God is to feel for me, or to forgive me my sins and offer me new life and happiness, but to invite me to become like God and to show the same compassion to others as he is showing to me."[3]

The radicality of Jesus' command allows us to overcome the impossible because it comes with a solution. Love (and forgive) others, even as God has loved (and forgiven) you. God never gives us orders without at the same time giving us the tools with which to carry out the order. That is the basis on which we can forgive the unforgivable, which includes the forgiveness of ourselves.

Notes

1. James, H. (1986). *The Wings of a Dove.* New York: Viking Press.

2. Nouwen, H. (1994). *The Return of the Prodigal Son: A Meditation on Fathers, Brothers, and Sons.* New York: Doubleday, p. 125.

3. Ibid. p. 115.

Forgiveness and Transformation

Brendan Walsh

"We've heard the truth. There is even talk about forgiveness and reconciliation. But where's the justice?"
—Testimony to South Africa's Truth and Reconciliation Commission

"Can't you see the dolphins? Aren't they magnificent? Look!"

I peered past my host's pointing finger to the horizon, where a white foamy crust was appearing on the sea's surface. I had to take Jane's word for it on the dolphins. Jane was a former ballet dancer who had come to South Africa for a holiday fifteen years ago and decided to stay, an astonishingly common story. Now she helps cushion the effects of the crumbling Rand by working odd mornings for a friend who runs a bed and breakfast place in the Western Cape. "This is the most beautiful place in the world," she told me. "And," she added, catching her breath, "surely the strangest."

Below us several holiday homes and exclusive guesthouses were planted amongst the dense thickets of milkwood and candlewood trees on steep cliffs leading down to a sandy beach. Africa ends in an exhilarating sliver of coastline, known to its original inhabitants as *Outeniqua* ("the man laden with honey"). The Khoikhoi were quickly scooped aside by white settlers in an early episode in what became a 350-year brutal, unforgiving, and largely one-sided, struggle for ownership of this land and control of its fruits.

47

We watched as the gardeners appeared to begin work for the day, and maids in blue nurses' uniforms swept clean the terracotta patios and unfurled the sun loungers. Eventually, white couples emerged in dark glasses to take up their stations by the swimming pools.

In South Africa, five years after the first democratic elections of 1994 and the transition to majority rule, everything is different, and everything is the same. Something extraordinary has happened. A country that teetered on the brink of a violent cataclysm for decades somehow hauled itself to a peaceful accommodation while the world, and South Africans themselves, gaped in astonishment and relief. In the five years since the miracle—to use the inescapable cliché—of Nelson Mandela's transformation from political prisoner to state president, South Africa has created a carefully balanced constitutional framework that protects the rights of all its citizens. South Africans are now free from forced removals, able to pass laws, and have joined those who are free to choose those whom they wish to govern them. Clean water, improved electricity supplies, and telephone lines have been brought to the townships, and free school meals are supplied every day to millions of children. Though the euphoria of 1994 has been replaced by a mood of wariness, frustration, and uncertainty, the fragile mutual trust between politicians and citizens necessary for a stable government has been stretched but not broken. Remarkably, the process continues. "Given the scale of the task," as one analyst summed up the new government's achievement, "progress has been limited but nonetheless remarkable."[1]

Yet South Africa remains as bizarrely askew as it was five years ago. There are a few more blacks driving BMWs and a few more whites begging in the streets. But for the most part, it is still the whites who relax by the pool while the black maids sweep the floors. South Africa remains a tense, deeply fractured society, with its communities having little stake in each others' failures and successes.

The twenty-minute journey from the airport into Cape Town is a startling and disturbing reminder of the persistence of South Africa's deep divisions. A three-lane highway with familiar bottle-green road signs and "three-two-one" countdown markers that indicate the slipway rolls toward the shopping malls, luxury hotels, seafood restaurants, and beaches that lie at the foot of Table Mountain. Yet beyond the fences on either side are sprawling townships where families share murky one-room shoebox homes. Jobs here are as hard as ever to come by, and healthcare and schooling are no less fitful and elusive than before the transition. Ask people if life has changed for the better since 1994 and you tend to be told, "We're worse off than ever." People here are quietly angry. "The money has stayed just where it has always been," Margaret, a young mother of six told me, gesturing upwards, "at the top."

A priest working in one of the colored townships—where thousands of families were forcibly resettled in the 1960s during apartheid's purge of Cape Town's "black spots"—reckoned that 40 percent of the men of working age in his parish were unemployed. "It creates frustration and despair, and, sure enough, these are the families where there is drug abuse and domestic violence."

White people complain that education and health standards are starting to slide. They are unhappy that they are no longer as spectacularly privileged in employment prospects and the provision of services as they once were in relation to the majority. They are infuriated by the restlessness shown by the government at the continued absence of black and colored players in the national rugby and cricket teams. The Afrikaner seems prepared, under protest, to swallow affirmative action for bankers and lawyers; but the prospect of affirmative action for rugby players sticks in his throat. Privately, though, the whites will admit, a little to their astonishment, that life goes on much as before.

The tenseness and unease are palpable. Almost everyone talks incessantly about the increasing crime rate and shares horror stories of attacks on remote farmers and rapes and muggings in city centers in broad daylight. White homes, their walls topped with razor wire, increasingly resemble fortresses, regularly patrolled by armed security guards.

We inhabit a world large enough and are blessed with imaginations obtuse enough to live largely untroubled by the crass imbalances of security, wealth, and opportunity that exist

49

between us, but it is impossible not to be shaken by the scene of the gardeners, the maids, and their employers—the raw truth of the separate and different grooves of their lives still in place in spite of the extraordinary upheaval of apartheid's collapse. Nevertheless, this is the way the world works. We do unspeakable things to each other; we sicken of the horrors or grow weary from our quarrels; we make a kind of lopsided peace; and somehow we settle down again to live and work together, cheek by jowl, with our hands still bloodied and our wounds still raw, half-reconciled and half-resentful: black and white, men and women, parents and children.

This is a story I heard late one evening in a smoky bar in Ireland. It has gone round and round in my head for nearly thirty years. It was told to me by Michael, like me a pale-faced English boy on holiday with his Irish relations. We were both sixteen or seventeen, an age when the consumption of alcohol is more a matter of honor than of enjoyment. Three summers previously, Michael had been swimming with friends when one of the boys got into difficulties. He seemed to panic and, instead of conserving his energies, began screaming and waving wildly. Then quite suddenly, he slipped beneath the waves and the commotion stopped. Michael and the others frantically called out their friend's name and splashed around in the water in desperation. The boy's body was recovered the following day. Michael was stunned and consumed by guilt. His friends, his teachers, and his parents all assured him that there was nothing more he could have done, that the current was strong and had taken another boy's life the previous summer, and that there were several other people there and none of them had behaved any differently. Even the dead boy's father told him that if he had tried to swim out to try to save their son he too would have been swept away, and there would have been two grieving mothers, rather than one.

Still, Michael kept going over and over the events of that afternoon. He knew he could have done more, and the knowledge gnawed away at him. Then he met a priest who heard his story. The priest listened and said he could understand why Michael felt he had let himself and his friend down. He did not put any blame on Michael for what had happened, but neither did he try to reassure Michael that he had done the best he reasonably could. He told Michael that if he told God he was truly sorry for failing to do his best, he would be forgiven.

Michael said, "It was the first time someone had not tried to comfort me or find an explanation for what I had done. But what he said seemed to help more than anything. I still feel bad, but it's sort of OK now."

The priest had not said much, it seemed to me. He had simply told Michael that whatever had happened, it was all in God's hands now.

The experience of forgiveness is infinitely precious. I suppose I can look back on the same undistinguished track record of squandered opportunities, wheedling compromises, and petty betrayals that litter most lives. The closest shaves I have had with the ways of God have been less experiences of enlightenment or inspiration than of disembarkation, of leaving some of the bad stuff in God's hands: the clumsy bruising of those who have loved me the most, the half-baked and ham-fisted apologies, the uninventive way I repeat the same mistakes over and over. Forgiveness allows us to remember our betrayals without being destroyed by them. We are released from the need to ransack the archives to find the missing clue to our past mistakes, to trace our failures back to some quirk of social engineering, an incident on the school playground, or an unlucky shuffle of our genetic inheritance. I wonder, of course, if it is just a comforting trick we play on ourselves. Yet I am able to take a deep breath and say, "Oh, Brendan, you screwed up badly there." And I wonder—and the image of God as a sort of hotel porter is not, I know, terribly theologically sophisticated—how people cope with no one to take care of all their baggage.

Seeking and offering forgiveness is an uncomfortable exchange. At one end of the relationship, the receiving end, there is shame and embarrassment—the admission of past selfishness or cruelty. It is not easy to identify oneself as belonging to the giving end of forgiveness, either—a reminder of one's place in the dreary drama of exploitation: first, the humiliated, bullied, or abused one, then the plucky survivor, until finally, in another unglamorous role, the patient and forgiving one. Though forgiveness is a currency few enjoy dealing in, we could not live in a world in which we received our just desserts. We are too imperfect, and we let each other down too often. We have to allow ourselves to write off our debts. Only by forgiving ourselves can living with ourselves be possible, and only by forgiving others and being forgiven by them is living in communities possible.

But how do we forgive well? How do we remember without being weighed down by the awfulness of the past? How do we move on without forgetting what we must learn from the mistakes of the past? This is at the heart of living well, for individuals and for societies.

The Chairperson of South Africa's Truth and Reconciliation Commission (TRC), Archbishop Desmond Tutu, described Fr. Michael Lapsley as an "icon of what the TRC stands for." Lapsley was seriously injured in a letter bomb attack in 1990. "I realised," he wrote later, "that if I became filled with hatred and a desire for revenge, I would remain a victim forever." Lapsley made up his mind not to forget his experience but not to be destroyed by it either. "I asked myself, why did I survive a bomb that was supposed to kill me? Perhaps to be a sign that love and faith and gentleness are stronger than hatred and evil and death."[2]

"If we recognise our woundedness," suggests Lapsley, "heal our memories and move towards wholeness, then we have a much greater chance of breaking the cycle and creating a different type of society."[3] Lapsley's prescription for his personal recovery echoes the spirit of Tutu's vision for the TRC's contribution to national recovery after the violent trauma of the apartheid years.

When the TRC's hearings opened in East London on the Eastern Cape in April 1996, South Africa was still just waking up to its inevitable hangover. There was enough euphoria left for the Commission to make a tacit assumption that if the true story of the past could be told and acknowledged, reconciliation would follow. At first, the commissioners simply asked the witnesses to tell them what happened. "We will find out the truth, and the truth will lead to reconciliation."

Over two and a half years, some twenty-one thousand people came forward to make submissions, over two thousand of them appearing in person to tell their own individual story at public hearings held throughout the country. The effect was dramatic and devastating. One white woman told me how she frequently wept with horror and shame as she listened, night after night, to the harrowing testimonies of survivors that were broadcast on the radio. Before the TRC, it was common for whites to claim that accusations against the police and security forces regarding acts of violence and torture were fabricated or grossly exaggerated. Since the TRC hearings, it is said that it is terrible that these abuses took place—but we never knew about them.

For many of the survivors, for victims and their families, simply being allowed to tell their story, often a story suppressed or denied for many years, was a grim but powerful and healing experience. Simply to uncover the truth, or more of the truth, has been one of the TRC's most important achievements.

Producing an outcome that is both just and sustainable, especially in the South African context, where the "accused" still carry such power, has been immensely sensitive and complex— and it has carried a price. The TRC's priority was to discover what really happened rather than to allocate blame or hand out punishments or rewards. As Tutu remarked, it had to perform a juggling act "between those who want amnesia and those who want retribution." The TRC was given the impossibly difficult task of so carefully nudging the truth to the surface that the needs of the survivors, and of society, for truth-telling and hearing the story would be satisfied without setting off a landslide of guilt, shame, anger, and retribution. If justice alone were allowed to take its course, Tutu observed, the country would be reduced to ashes. The TRC opted instead for an imperfect truth and an imperfect justice. It had little choice.

Stability, inclusiveness, and the maintenance of national unity—grand words for continuing the grueling process—have been the post-apartheid government's overriding goals. It has put reconciliation above restitution and redistributed wealth so tentatively that whites squeal but do not run, while blacks grumble but do not revolt. Perhaps these priorities simply reflect the characteristic values of our age. We put stability and inclusiveness ahead of justice and fairness. Narratives of compromise and reconciliation are perfect for an age marked by tolerance and pluralism and allergic to overarching ideologies or systems. Rather than seek for what is true or false, just or unfair, we look for what works, what people will live with. We try, as we say on the morning after a management-training weekend, to learn from what happened and "close it down," so that we can "move on." We seek no-blame, win-win solutions.

In return for the truth, the TRC has granted amnesty to the perpetrators of crimes—the secular version of forgiveness. But as many of the survivors have pointed out, forgiveness is not something that can be granted by proxy. Only the one who has suffered is entitled to grant forgiveness. Some of the victims of apartheid and their families who had testified to the TRC told the writer Timothy Garton Ash, "We don't like this. Only we have the right to forgive, and we're not yet ready to."[4]

There is something sour and devalued about a forgiveness that is coerced. Forgiveness has to be freely given to be of value. The TRC emerged from the long, drawn out process of creating a deal for a hand over of power from the governing white minority to the black majority. At the close of the bitterly fought Boer War, Jan Smuts agreed to make terms with the British rather than fight to the bitter end, arguing that it was better to "negotiate an orderly peace now under the best possible terms than to be crushed later and have ignominious terms thrust upon us."[5] More than ninety years later, state president F. W. de Klerk reached a similar conclusion. White economists had earlier made the calculation that the costs of preserving apartheid were starting to outweigh whatever perceived benefits there might be to racial segregation. And so, as one commentator put it, the people with the money and the people with the numbers got together and made a deal.[6]

By acting while still ahead, the leaders of the old regime were able to negotiate the terms of their own defeat—and a crucial element in the agreement they secured from the future rulers of South Africa was immunity from prosecution for their crimes. They were not powerful enough to secure, though, immunity from an investigation into the truth about the past. Mandela and the African National Congress had insufficient power at the negotiating table to ensure the perpetrators would be prosecuted, but they were able to demand truth in exchange for amnesty. In order to secure a negotiated settlement rather than force a prolonged war of liberation, they agreed to trade justice for the truth.

To many observers, it seemed that the representatives of the police and security forces who applied to the TRC for amnesty in return for the truth were proffering their disclosures like men cashing in a check in exchange for a new car. As the final report of the TRC commented, "Even where political leaders of the former state claimed to take full responsibility for the actions of the past, these sometimes seemed to take the form of ritualised platitudes rather than genuine expressions of remorse."[7]

When the granting of forgiveness is reduced to bartering, it loses its savor. Former National Party minister Leon Wessells was one of the few perpetrators who seemed to grasp the moment, offering a rare and eloquent heartfelt apology, "I am now more convinced than ever that apartheid was a terrible mistake that blighted our land. South Africans did not listen to the laughing and crying of each other. I am sorry that I had been so hard of hearing for so long."

The TRC process has done much to help bring understanding, healing and wholeness to South African communities. Yet many of the survivors and victims have been left hurt and angered by the process, feeling that—once again—they have been used, this time as pawns in some wider game. The TRC process has asked of those who were tortured or imprisoned or who lost their loved ones, those who have already suffered the most, to bear the greatest sacrifice: to forgive without receiving justice in return, for the sake of "the national interest."

In my Catholic upbringing, I understood that doing selfish, wicked, and foolish things is, well, it is what people do. The interesting thing, the thing that makes the difference, is what they do next. That I would steal apples or sneak a look at a brighter pupil's examination paper was to be expected, but confessing, owning up honestly when found out, was a key part, almost the defining act, of "being good." Taking responsibility, the admission of guilt, this was the important thing. There was talk too, of course, of words like "reparation." I had to do more than "say sorry." I had to repair the wrong, to replace the stolen goods. I was contracted to do better in the future—to make "a firm purpose of amendment."

John the Baptist delivered a chilling rebuke to the Pharisees when they appeared at the river Jordan, looking to be baptized, "You brood of vipers! Who warned you to flee from the coming wrath?" He sent them away with the angry warning to make sure they "produce fruit in keeping with repentance" (Matthew 3:7-8 NIV).

A loose reading of the story of the scapegoat in Leviticus might look like an example of reconciliation disengaged from transformation: "Then Aaron shall lay both his hands on the head of the live goat, and confess over it all the iniquities of the people of Israel, and all their transgressions, all their sins, putting them on the head of the goat, and sending it away into the wilderness . . . " (Leviticus 16:21). But the crucial point of the holy day of Yom Kippur (Atonement) is not only that the sins of the community are acknowledged, but that their symbolic banishment is indissolubly linked to the transition to a new order, in which God's people commit to leave their old ways and live by a new set of laws.

From the time of his election in 1978, Pope John Paul II began to wind himself up for the millennium. At the center of his preparations, he has put repentance and conversion. This is more than mere truth-telling. There could be no true celebration of the millennium without first putting the wrongs of the past right. Thus, the Pope has boldly led calls for the remission of debt owed by poor countries. It is not enough to acknowledge the failures and omissions of the past, to apologize, as is increasingly fashionable, for the sins of the past.

Confession must be backed up by action. The Church "cannot cross the threshold of the new millennium without encouraging her children to purify themselves, through repentance, of past errors and instances of infidelity, inconsistency and slowness to act."[8]

In South Africa, as deputy president Thabo Mbeki has said, "reconciliation must be more than just sharing tea." Everyone recognizes that forgiveness and reconciliation are an indispensable part of the healing of the divisions in South African society. Everyone recognizes that making a significant and lasting change in a climate of fear and incomprehension that has been gathering momentum for centuries will take many years, perhaps generations. The TRC has made an outstanding start, but it has been a reminder that a forgiveness that is coerced, out of fear or exhaustion or calculation, will be hollow. A forgiveness that is reduced to a glib formula of "forgive and forget" will only create more resentment. When reconciliation hides (perhaps even from the actors themselves) the truth that the underlying flaw—the unjust power relation—remains intact, it becomes an empty performance. If forgiveness is not to be the final demeaning admission of one's relationship to one's oppressor—always the one under pressure, always the one who is being asked to give something—it has to be linked to conversion, to the promotion of justice, and to the redistribution of wealth and power. Better honest bitterness than a sham reconciliation.

Mrs. Kondile was one of the many witnesses to the Commission who remains unreconciled, unable to forgive her son's murderer. A few hours earlier the accused had described to the Commission his labored immolation of her son's body with a trainspotter's precision, "The burning of a body takes seven hours. The fleshier parts of the body take longer. . . . That's why we frequently had to turn the buttocks and thighs of Kondile." It was just another horror story in what often seemed an eternal serial telling of atrocities. "It is easy for Mandela and Tutu to forgive," said Mrs. Kondile. "They lead vindicated lives. In my life nothing, not a single thing, has changed since my son was burned by barbarians . . . nothing. Therefore I cannot forgive."

Notes

1. *South Africa: Breaking New Ground* (1996). London: Catholic Institute for International Relations.

2. Lapsley, M. (1995). *My Journey of Reconciliation: From Freedom Fighter to Healer*, p. 4.

3. Michael Lapsley, quoted in *Pietermaritzburg Agency for Christian Social Awareness Newsletter* 62, Easter 1995, p. 4. Both the Lapsley quotations are also found in Brian Frost, *Struggling to Forgive*, London, 1998.

4. *The Observer*. May 16, 1998.

5. *South African Times*. December 14, 1994.

6. Frederick van Zyl Slabbert, former leader of the Progressive Party.

7. The full text of the Truth and Reconciliation Committee is published in five volumes. It is available on the Internet at www.truth.org.za.

8. John Paul II, (1994). *Tertio Millennio Adveniente: Preparation for the Jubilee of the Year 2000*. London: Catholic Truth Society.

How to Lose One's Temper and Find It Again

Monica Furlong

I grew up in a kindly middle-class British household where the expression of anger by the adults, and to an extent by the children, was taboo. The odd tightening of the lips, the glare, the huffiness, the occasional banging of saucepans, they were all there, but the actual putting of the feelings into words was not permitted. I suspect that this was not unusual in families of my era and background. Of course, the taboo worked at some human cost. Such powerful feelings as anger, inevitable when a family spends a lot of time together, do not simply evaporate. In my parents' case they took their toll in stomach ulcers, constant migraines, or feelings of fatigue and unwellness. My sister was given to what would probably be diagnosed now as psychosomatic illnesses, and I had a stammer. Stammering has a quite complicated causation and cannot be attributed to a single determinant, but I have no doubt that discovering that you are not permitted to express powerful feelings at about the period when you are learning to talk often comes into it somewhere.

But any taboo is always interesting and secretly exciting, and my family history had the bizarre effect on me in that I have always found people who lose their tempers absolutely fascinating and have loved having a ringside seat for the occasion. My father lost his temper exactly twice in the whole of my childhood—with considerable provocation each time—and I found it thrilling and wished he would do it more often. I think it made me feel safer. It made him seem more human, and it meant that whatever I had done that made him angry was not as terrible as it had been in my imagination. (Yes, I do know that many children have a very different experience and have to live with frightening adults who are always losing their tempers, but it does not alter the fact that in my case a little more openness about feelings, particularly anger, would have been a good thing.)

For years I was so well-conditioned that I never lost my temper and was never even mildly rude to people who were rude to me. A bad-tempered shop assistant would have me sniffing back tears, until one day, marvelous to tell, I surprised myself by snapping back a smart reply. The effect, for me, was miraculous. The stammer vanished (temporarily), I felt wonderful, and suddenly I could see that there was an alternative to putting up weakly with nastiness from other people.

It was not an immediate cure; it has taken me the rest of my life to learn to say when I am angry, let alone to do so while I am still feeling fairly calm, but these early experiences left me with a considerable respect for anger. Of course, there are degrees of it. Some small slights from other people (for instance, drivers who behave badly on the road) may arouse our fury, but they will inevitably fade quickly from our minds. Only fairly mad people let small slights blow up into the fantasy of a major insult. It would be idle to deny, however, that people, particularly among family, friends, and lovers perhaps, injure one another quite seriously at times, because we all place so much investment in love and trust and are also quite frightened of commitment and possession. Anger may be "legitimate" in some such situations, and the recovery from these times may not be quick or easy.

The first thing to be said about anger, however, whether it is repressed or expressed, is that it is extraordinarily powerful—one of the great human sources of energy and action. This means that in certain times and seasons, it is a very useful engine—most reformers are driven by an engine of anger which they use to make life better for others. There are dangers of a sickening self-righteousness combined with a one-sided way of seeing the world, however, around all that—and those who work in areas of reform have to be careful to balance their lives with other concerns and, above all, with loving relationships, but the great engine of anger must not be wasted. We have to learn to use its power for good and not for destruction, and that is a subtle and little understood art.

The second thing to realize is that anger is a very important indicator in a relationship. Just as physical pain usefully warns us that we are sick or in danger of damaging our bodies, anger warns us that a relationship between us and another person or group of persons is beginning to go wrong; perception and action are urgently needed.

You will understand that, given this history of respect for anger, I feel uncomfortable around those, often Christian, who share my parents' terror of it. I believe that a certain kind of deadness sets in where people will not or cannot express anger, that it makes true fellowship impossible and encourages underhanded methods of emitting rage. For instance, I have come across more backbiting in church circles, where direct expression of anger is often inhibited, than in the world of newspapers and broadcasting—supposedly less "moral"—where I earned my living for many years. People who are not trying so hard to "be good" often seem able to be more generous with one another's faults and failures. I have not forgotten a particular religious order I stayed with once that worked off an enormous amount of displaced anger by complaining that others had not cleaned the bath properly or that others were not as ill as they were pretending to be (and I have never lived with any group of people who were so frequently sick in bed).

All this has tended to make me a bit nervous when people talk too freely about forgiveness. It is not that I do not think it is desirable or necessary or that I do not see the tragedy of a world where certain communities revel in hatred, but I fear the temptation to pretend a forgiveness that is not truly felt, the apparent renunciation of an anger that continues to seethe inside all the time. I find that the friends and family I continue to love and have close relationships with are the ones who are capable of knowing and expressing their anger. Those who will not tell me about any negative feeling leave me nervous and incapable of trusting. Anger is not, in my experience, that easy to reach and disperse; I distrust those who cannot even admit that there is a problem.

Yet, in the last few years, several things have happened that made me feel I must move on to a new place, to see if I can find my way to a more positive sense of forgiveness. One of them is observing people who have been unable to forgive and the mess it has made of their lives. I think of P, for example, whose husband left her for another woman many years ago. P was still quite young. She might have resumed the successful career she abandoned when she had children, continued to enjoy her children, and even married again. Instead her life revolved around her bitterness, until it made the life of others bitter, too, and gradually drove family and friends away from her. She must have felt that if she forgave D she would crumble—her life would have no more meaning. But it seemed to her children that she wanted her former husband to continue to suffer indefinitely—never to be allowed to forget the injury he had done to her. Instead, of course, it was she who suffered most.

J cut himself off from his parents as an undergraduate, never wrote or telephoned or went to see them. I do not know what effect it had on them, nor quite what they had done to merit this treatment (and it may have been something terrible), but J himself seemed, to me, wounded and diminished by this choice, much as P had been. It was as if he could not leave his parents behind: he was always thinking about them, even though he never saw them. They dominated his life by their absence.

In contrast there was E who had been taken to a concentration camp as an adolescent boy in the late years of World War II. He was still very young when he came out, physically and psychologically frail after his terrible ordeal. He told me that he spent months simply hating the Nazis and what they had done to him and his family. "It took up all my energy!" Perhaps, at first, he needed that just to hold him together in his misery. Then one day, he told me, it struck him that this was hurting him more than it hurt them. "On that day I went to the university and registered as a student. Life went on."

Another thing that affected my understanding of forgiveness was an injury that somebody did to me many years ago, an injury by anyone's standard. For several years I went over it daily, raging to myself and feeling the pain of it. After ten years, though it had abated quite a lot, I found myself telling a psychoanalyst about it and how I did not feel I had entirely forgiven the incident. "Perhaps you never will," she said. I am not quite sure why, but this remark was oddly liberating. From that day the anger gradually seeped away, and when I eventually went back to think about it all once more, I found that the wound had healed. I was sorry the incident had happened—it had left a scar—but I was past it now, in another place altogether.

Another experience was of being deeply, and it seemed arbitrarily, wounded by a friend I was staying with. Moving from there to another friend, I poured the whole story out, somewhat tearfully. The second friend listened gratifyingly hard and agreed that I had been badly treated, but then she said, "Now, let it go. Otherwise you will be doing exactly what X is doing—making a mountain out of a molehill." There was something liberating in her saying this to me. It had not occurred to me before that it was possible to make a leap out of a tangle of hurt feelings; I had always ruminated ceaselessly on my injuries until finally exhaustion set in. It was a moment of insight about forgiveness. It meant trying to stop myself from getting into the myself-as-victim, poor-old-me mode and recognizing that some sort of creepy game was going on between myself and X but that I did not have to play.

Crucial consideration in the area of forgiveness is needed in regard to the people, usually friends, who have forgiven me, usually for neglecting them or sometimes for wronging them, and have done so joyfully, without reproach, and without a trace of contaminating anger. This has not been a frequent occurrence—it is not, and should not be, in anyone's life—but when it has happened to me it has seemed magical, moving, and divinely powerful because it was done without any lust for power. For me, it established a deep root of trust in friends who were capable of so much love. It reminded me that love and goodness are the most beautiful things in the world and are always so deeply original and true that, like a work of genius, they are inexplicable in ordinary human terms. To be forgiven is to get a glimpse of God.

The world offers amazing examples of people capable of extraordinary acts of generosity almost beyond my imagining. I have only to think of Nelson Mandela and how his humanness not only survived but triumphed over a brutal regime and a dehumanizing prison. W. H. Auden once suggested that it is important to honor what he called the "vertical," or righteous, man—however "horizontal" many of us, men and women, may know ourselves to be.[1] The vertical Mandela, the vertical Bonhoeffer, and others, known only to us as friends and mentors, show that there is an alternative to soldiering on with our rage, though it is not easy to see exactly how it works.

Earlier this year I visited the Corrymeela Community—that nucleus of hope in Northern Ireland—where, since the late 1960s, they have worked and lived with the broken and the bereaved and talked the language of forgiveness in the face of hatred and unspeakable atrocity. I put my bald and rather obvious question to one of their staff, whom I knew to have great experience with the terrain. "What do you do if you just can't get on with someone?" "You don't have to like them. You just have to wish them well in their life."

I was ready to hear this because it put its finger exactly on the spot where I always get stuck when I feel wronged: the tendency to obsess about what they did and what I did and to spiral off into self-justification. Suddenly I saw at least a partial solution; it might be possible to break the spiral and simply wish the person well and get on with my life.

A personal and collective movement of that kind may be our only hope, the corrective to the rage and fanaticism and bitter memories of which human beings are all too capable, and which, in the short term or as much as several hundred years later, wreak appalling acts of destruction. We can make up our minds not to nourish hatred and not to join groups that do.

At Corrymeela the great Ray Davey told me how, after his experiences as a German prisoner in the Second World War, he saw the need for reconciliation. As a student chaplain in the post-war period, he took groups of students to Italy and Germany, and on one of these trips, they met Karl Barth. "What should we do to promote world peace, sir?" one student asked. "Go home and put your own house in order," came the reply. Ray Davey went home and, together with his wife Kathleen and friends who shared their vision, started the Corrymeela Community.

Over the door as you leave Corrymeela are the words "Corrymeela begins when you leave" to remind you that life is all about reconciliation. Not a bad motto, especially for angry people like me. And us.

Note

1. Auden, W. H. (1966). *The Collected Shorter Poems of W. H. Auden: 1927–1957*. London: Faber and Faber, p. 43.

Forgiveness: The Final Form of Love

Donald J. Shelby

J ohn Wesley, the founder of Methodism, went to the colony of Georgia as a missionary to the Native Americans after graduating from Oxford University and being ordained as an Anglican priest. At one point, Wesley interceded with Governor Oglethorpe on behalf of a man Wesley deemed wrongly charged with breaking the law. In a perhaps apocryphal account, Wesley asked Oglethorpe to forgive the man, but Oglethorpe responded, "I never forgive!" Wesley replied, "Then, sir, I hope you never sin."

Wesley could well have added, "I hope, sir, that you never want to love or be loved." Because forgiveness and love belong together. Indeed, forgiveness makes love possible. To love and to be loved is to forgive again and again and again.

It is clear why this is so. Every human being has a shadow side and is full of limitations and contradictions. We humans are driven by erratic compulsions and have irrational, unpredictable responses that we do not understand and many times cannot control. Human life is also situational. It is always lived a certain place, with certain people, in a certain moment of time, and it can be frustrating as well as fulfilling.

Moreover, there is an innate distance between people. People are always, in part, a mystery to each other—separate and remote. While having a unique history and genetic composition, with different points of reference, perspectives, and personalities, people still come together seeking to relate to one another, to share life space, and to love one another. They attempt to communicate and to understand one another, but messages between them are often not completed; misunderstandings

67

arise, wrong assumptions are made, and people are left feeling threatened and resentful. Defenses are raised, anger flares, and people attack one another with ugly words and physical violence. People reject and injure one another, demean and condemn one another, and distance themselves and try to destroy one another. No-man's-lands are created between people—bleak wastelands of nursed grievances, suspicions, distortion, and estrangement. What is true between individual people is also true for groups, for institutions, and for nations. Warfare among nations, tragic conflict and internecine struggles within nations, massacres, hate crimes, structures of injustice, abridgment of human rights, ethnic cleansing, and wasted resources and energies are the dreadful consequences of loss of community and loss of love.

Only forgiveness can overcome that loss as people take the risk and move into the no-man's-lands between them and actively seek reconciliation and restoration of community and love. Someone enters the wasteland of estrangement and says, "I am sorry, please forgive me and take me back," and someone else closes the gap by responding, "You are forgiven." Only then is love possible once more; only then can people grow on together.

If we have offended someone else or betrayed a covenant, trivialized a relationship or violated someone else's integrity, all we can do is step into the wasteland, move toward the offended, and say, "I am sorry, please forgive me." In asking to be forgiven, in saying it, feeling it, and affirming it, we indicate that we want the relationship to be restored. With such an act of penitence, we signal our readiness and desire to do whatever is necessary to bring healing, make restitution, and move beyond the hostility and brokenness in order to explore a renewed relationship of deeper constancy and intimacy. To say "Please forgive me" is to commit to receive forgiveness if it is offered (it may not be), to forgive ourselves and to reverence, humbly, being forgiven as a gift. To seek forgiveness makes possible reconciliation, the healing of memory, and the rebirth of love.

To offer forgiveness to someone who seeks it completes the joy of reconciliation. To forgive someone who has offended, wronged, or betrayed us is to offer ourselves once again in spite of what has happened. To forgive is not to forget, as the theologian Paul Tillich reminds us, correcting that conventional wisdom. Instead, to forgive is to open ourselves again in trust while still remembering how trust was betrayed. To forgive is to invite those who have rejected and hurt us to be close again in order to create a restored relationship with them.

Forgiveness cannot and does not change what happened, no matter how serious or disruptive. What has happened has happened; what was said cannot be retracted. Forgiveness is instead a deliberate change of attitude about what has happened. It is an intentional decision to change how we feel about what happened and what it means for us. Forgiveness creates, therefore, the possibility for a future together, the opportunity to grow in love and faith together, and the realization of the potential that such bonding opens to us.

This truth was beautifully illustrated in the concluding segment of the acclaimed series, *The Civil War*, produced and directed by Ken Burns on public television. People reported watching it with tears in their eyes. The theme of forgiveness and reconciliation was struck again and again as the series was brought to a close. The final scenes were almost mythic, showing us how reconciliation and forgiveness elicit the "better angels of our nature," how loving and being loved show forth human greatness.

The same discovery has come to estranged husbands and wives who took the risk to seek forgiveness or give it and then claimed the dynamics of reconciliation and created a new future for their relationship. It has also come to families where trust has been betrayed and grievances have been nursed into hatred until someone took the initiative to effect reconciliation and restore the family bond. The discovery has come to grieving parents who mourn the death of a son or daughter in a fatal accident, but who forgive the person responsible for the accident. The awakening has reunited hostile professional colleagues and restored friendships ruined by exploitation and bitterness.

In such moments, when forgiveness is sought, offered, and received, and reconciliation begins, we are in touch with our higher nature and experience a transcendent dimension of love. That is why Reinhold Niebuhr wrote, "The only whole relation-

69

ship is a healed one; therefore, forgiveness is the final form of love."[1] And Nobel Laureate Albert Camus pointed to it when he declared, "No ultimacy or creativity lies in hatred or contempt. In some corner of the heart, at some moment in history, the creative person ends by reconciling."[2]

Not surprisingly, the scriptures of all the major world religions make such reconciliation a moral imperative and hold the experience as a paradigm of the divine/human relationship desired by God. From the bold cadences of the Hebrew prophets to the soaring exhortations on love in the Bhagavad Gita of Hinduism, from a similar summons in the wisdom of Buddha and the concept of the bodhisattva way of life to the teachings of Jesus, the message is the same. Forgiveness and love belong together because God creates human life so that its greatest meaning is found in both. Moreover, in forgiveness and love, human beings experience the presence and purpose of God at work in the world and in human lives. The dying Jesus prays from the cross for his tormentors and executioners, "Father, forgive them, for they know not what they do," and we realize such forgiveness is the final form of love as God intended it. Love and forgiveness belong together. You cannot have one without the other. As the Christian scripture sings:

> Beloved, let us love one another, because love is from God; everyone who loves is born of God and knows God. . . . Those who say, "I love God" and hate their brothers and sisters, are liars; for those who do not love a brother or sister whom they have seen, cannot love God whom they have not seen. The commandment we have from him is this: those who love God must love their brothers and sisters also. (1 John 4:7, 20-21)

Adolfo Perez Esquivel, Nobel Peace Prize winner, was imprisoned by the military dictatorship in Argentina and spent eighteen months in solitary confinement. He felt anger, outrage, and depression but ultimately determined he would not seek revenge and try to kill his oppressors if he were set free. Instead, he would work at bringing a new order into being, where life would be sacred and people would live in peace and dignity. In the months after his release from prison, Perez Esquivel was haunted by Jesus' words, "Father, forgive them, for they know not what they do." To Perez Esquivel, the words made no sense, for his torturers had known exactly what they were doing, but suddenly it dawned on him: what his torturers did not know, what they were entirely ignorant of, was that humanity is *one*, that we are brothers and sisters in the family of God. What his torturers did *not* know was that Perez Esquivel was *not* an enemy they were torturing, but a *brother*. Perez Esquivel concluded that the only way he could communicate that truth to them was to forgive them and to love them.[3] And he did.

Forgiveness is the final form of love!

Notes

1. Bingham, J. (1992). *Courage to Change: An Introduction to the Life and Thought of Reinhold Niebuhr*. Lanham, MD: University Press of America.

2. Camus, A. (1952). Preface in Oscar Wilde, *La Ballade de la Geole de Reading*. Jacques Bour (trans.). Paris: Falaize, p. 239.

3. Cane, B. (1992). *Circles of Hope*. Maryknoll, NY: Orbis Books, pp. 100-101.

The Double Binds of Forgiveness

Halbert D. Weidner

At the turn of the century, the American General "Black Jack" Pershing was a hero of my great-grandmother. When the United States entered World War I and Pershing led the American forces, my great-grandmother vilified him and never forgave him. She saw our entrance into the war as a rescue of the English and the English empire. She was a Scot named Molly McGregor Young. She named my grandfather after Rob Roy, a romanticized figure based on Robert McGregor, a symbol of Presbyterian resistance to the English. All on that side of the family were Presbyterian Scots, and all had come over to North America in the late 1740s after the defeat of the last Stuart at Culloden.

Today we know that Molly's attitude is typical of tragic international situations and yet has some merit to it. First of all, in much official literature the cause is trivialized as hopelessly romantic and nostalgic. Second, it is viewed as impossibly complicated and past restitution. But historical wrongs have a way of not disappearing, and the grievances of the Scots have not evaporated. The centralizing Tories of the United Kingdom received not one district majority in Scotland, and the new Labour government is allowing power to devolve from London back north to Edinburgh. After centuries of centralization that deprived the Scots of proper self-determination, there is an adjustment that past wrongs demand. The attitude of nationalists in Scotland was fed by both hatred of the English and a legitimate grievance demanding restitution. Hatred never solves anything, but grievances can be mediated and something like justice achieved.

73

Molly faced one version of the double bind of forgiveness. All the spiritual traditions teach that anger and lack of forgiveness bind and destroy the sinned against as well as the aggressors. Not to forgive is to give greater power to the evil done to us by allowing the anger to do more harm to us. So there is the spiritually healing choice to forgive that unbinds the aggressor and the one who suffered the aggression.

The trouble with forgiveness, one evasion argues, is that it makes us too much like God. We probably would not mind being a god or goddess like Zeus or Aphrodite—something like a human being with an infinite capacity in some desired specialty like power or love. But to be like God—vulnerable, energized by such one-sided, infinite generosity—repels us. We can use this simple fact about forgiveness to avoid forgiving. We can be humble. Who am I to forgive? Only God can forgive! I leave the offender to God and retain my anger in all meekness. Spiritual traditions, Eastern and Western, agree that resisting forgiveness is easy and that to give in to the resistance reduces us.

The trouble with not forgiving is that it makes us less human. This is the other side of the double bind. The one who hurt us has really dumped a huge spiritual task on us. This task imposes a burden more difficult and more perilous than the original offense. Sometimes we can survive evil done to us but still not survive the trial of forgiving the evil. Such is the double burden of evil borne by the victim. If we have any tendency to be paralyzed by life's unfairness, the fear of this burden can sicken our capacity for growth. So to forgive is to become like God; not to forgive is to become less human. To be most human is to be most like God. That is the teaching of the common spiritual traditions. Standing in the way of this tradition is an ethic which teaches us that if we work hard and behave, everything will be all right. This is the common "good citizen" ethic that excludes the tragic element that will come to us all in the way of death and loss. Such an ethic makes life's goal the avoidance of suffering. Not all evil is banal, but banal people can be very evil if this ethic takes hold of ordinary people. It is not for nothing that in the West, there is a Christian tradition that includes both praying for the gift of forgiving others and being forgiven while at the same time praying for an escape from a time of trial and being delivered from evil.

It is understandable that forgiving is hard. It is legitimate to try to avoid being hurt so that we are not even placed in a position of needing to forgive. But when it cannot be avoided, then our freedom must come into play. Someone once said that freedom is what we use when we have no choices left. Stripped down to the bare experience of pain, suffering hurt and loss, our human freedom is engaged (some call this grace), and we forgive. We then emerge untouched in an essential way by the evil suffered. In fact, we emerge more human and, if more human, more like God.

But who needs this? Who wants it? In the wisdom tradition of the holy ones, the saints usually ask to be delivered from the worst spiritual challenges, such as having to forgive. They know they are too weak to stand up to the challenge. Not knowing what they might be called to face, however, they practice for the ultimate challenges like the forgiveness of others by learning not to judge others. The desert tradition in Christianity was emphatic about this. "Do not judge a fornicator if you are chaste, for if you do, you too are violating the law as much as he is. For he who said thou shalt not fornicate also said thou shalt not judge."[1] So one of the holy ones in the desert tells us. The mystic John of the Cross says simply, "If you do not want to be offended, don't take offense."

The second discipline was not clinging to possessions. This is very hard to understand in a country filled with lawsuits over property. Once a parent came to me asking for the lives of the saints for one of her children. I told her she was probably not interested in such a thing. She insisted after much discouragement from me. So I asked her what she would do if she came home and found the dining room furniture missing or half the clothes in the closet gone because her children had taken the lives of the saints seriously. The saints were not just good citizens. They certainly did not accumulate property or encourage it. Not having much leaves us with little that can be hurt. Not judging and not accumulating property that can be harmed leaves us free from most of the probable causes of needing to forgive others.

But what if all fails, and we are forced into a situation that requires us to acknowledge that we have been hurt and we need to forgive the offender? What does a prayer such as "forgive us our trespasses as we forgive those who trespass against us" mean to us then? To us, it seems that only Jesus, who taught us this prayer, could also live it. But there is supposed to be one saint in European history who was most like Jesus—Francis of Assisi. Francis is known as a great peacemaker.

No Franciscan or layperson accompanying a Franciscan was allowed to carry a weapon. Franciscans are most often in charge of Christian shrines in Muslim countries because they were known not to encourage crusades or any other kind of violence. Several companies of Franciscans were once slaughtered without defending themselves in order to prove that the followers of Francis were as peace-minded as he was. Francis is also lauded as a profound ecologist. In fact, he was. His sense of genuine unity with all creation is something not yet understood by the Western world. Francis was able to love and forgive everyone— except his own father. In renouncing worldly goods, he took his father's possessions and gave them away. He never asked forgiveness from his father. He never reconciled with him. Even within the perfection of this one great person, there is a profound resistance to forgiving, the one thing necessary to live a completely free life.

We embrace the task of forgiveness the same way we would embrace the choices forced on us by a disease like cancer. It is not something we want and the side effects are daunting, but we accept the reality of the disease and the cost of a cure. So we accept the fact that we have been wronged and that to hold on to the wrongs would be to die of the disease. We forgive and pay the price of forgiveness as we accept treatment and accept the side effects. We do not want the disease thrust on us, but we must accept the discipline of the cure once we have acknowledged the presence of the illness. The way out is to heal both of the double binds at the same time: the victim must take responsibility for the cure. The aggressor asking for forgiveness will not restore real peace, nor will the death of the aggressor. If the aggressors or their descendants eventually move in the direction of some kind of restitution, then part of the double bind can also be healed from the other side. But such justice does not bring back the dead or restore their lost future, so compensation fails in an essential way. Even when some kind of restitution is offered, only the forgiveness of the ones sinned against can restore a peace that honors the graves of the wronged. This is itself not fair, but in the unfairness we discover that reality, unjust as it is, raining on the good and the bad, is finally sacramental. The wound is healed first by forgiveness. Forgiveness takes a faith that is not very common, but faith healing is not routine, just the only way out.

Note

1. Merton, T., translator. (1960). *The Wisdom of the Desert: Sayings from the Desert Fathers of the Fourth Century.* Norfolk, CT: New Directions Books, p. 41.

Our Kind of Crowd

William H. Willimon

Then Peter came and said to him, "Lord, if another member of the church sins against me, how often should I forgive? As many as seven times?" Jesus said to him, "Not seven times, but, I tell you, seventy-seven times.

"For this reason the kingdom of heaven may be compared to a king who wished to settle accounts with his slaves. When he began the reckoning, one who owed him ten thousand talents was brought to him; and, as he could not pay, his lord ordered him to be sold, together with his wife and children and all his possessions, and payment to be made. So the slave fell on his knees before him, saying, 'Have patience with me, and I will pay you everything.' And out of pity for him, the lord of that slave released him and forgave him the debt. But that same slave, as he went out, came upon one of his fellow slaves who owed him a hundred denarii; and seizing him by the throat, he said, 'Pay what you owe.' Then his fellow slave fell down and pleaded with him, 'Have patience with me, and I will pay you.' But he refused; then he went out and threw him into prison until he would pay the debt. When his fellow slaves saw what had happened, they were greatly distressed and they went and reported to their lord all that had taken place. Then his lord summoned him and said to him, 'You wicked slave! I forgave you all that debt because you pleaded with me. Should you not have had mercy on your fellow slave, as I had mercy on you?' And in anger his lord handed him over to be tortured until he would pay his entire debt."
(Matthew 18:21-34)

D uring the Los Angeles riots in the aftermath of the first Rodney King verdict, Reginald Denny was dragged from his truck and viciously beaten by a raging gang. Payback time in L.A. After his painful recovery, he met face-to-face with his attackers, shook hands with them, and forgave them. A reporter, commenting on the scene, wrote, "It is said that Mr. Denny is suffering from brain damage."

There was a businessman who wished to settle up accounts, balance the books, set things in the right. So he called in his servants, among them one who owed "ten thousand talents" which is something like five tons of pure silver. We're talking big money.

Of course, there is no way to pay back such a fortune. Makes you feel real sorry for the little guy. The servant falls upon his knees sniveling something about patience and pity. The businessman has pity and writes off the whole debt. I will admit that this is not what they teach at the School of Business, but this is the Bible and strange things can happen. So this is a story of incredible debt incredibly forgiven.

This now forgiven servant goes out and happens to meet a fellow servant who owes him a few dollars. And he—remembering how much he has been forgiven—forgives his fellow servant his relatively small debt? Sure! Even though this is the Bible, there are limits to the strangeness. Now we get back to the real world. The once forgiven servant takes his fellow servant by the throat, hires a lawyer, and has him thrown into jail.

Word gets back to the boss about the way his once forgiven employee has acted. The boss calls him in, "You wicked slave! Look how much I forgave you! Whatever happened to mercy, pity, forgiveness?" So, of course, the businessman hands the little wretch over to his enforcer and the torture begins: broken legs, gouged eyes, shrieks and screams.

And Jesus says that the kingdom of God is somehow mixed up in that.

I do not know about the kingdom of God, but our kingdoms sure are. Debts must be paid. I, like you, hate to see anybody get away with anything. With whom do you identify in this story? The little servant who at first needs forgiving but, once forgiven, is none too forgiving? Or the king, the big businessman who at first forgives but, once he sees the real wretchedness of the one whom he has forgiven, ends the story with a scene straight from the movie *Pulp Fiction*?

One of the reasons Jesus tells these parables is that, in stories, we quite naturally apply them to ourselves. Jesus never says, "I'm going to tell you a story about a man who had a couple of sons, but it's really about you." He doesn't have to. We hear the story, we recognize our face, and we take our place in the narrative.

New Testament scholar Dan Via says that the parables of Jesus are like looking through the glass of a window. We look through the window at the world outside. The window is clear, therefore we see through the window to the world. But then there comes that moment when, looking through the window, we catch a reflection of ourselves in the glass. The parable becomes a mirror. We see ourselves.

Some of you are like the king in the story—powerful people to whom others incur great debts. Others of you, despite your efforts, are relatively powerless and you incur huge indebtedness to others. And whether you are in high or low places, there are many debts, and there will not be much mercy or pity.

Whether we are talking about the fancy homes where the bosses live on Country Club Way or the more modest row houses of the workers on Seventh Street—high or low—there is not much mercy. Forgiveness is in short supply. It only lasts for the first verse or two of the story, then it is back to retribution, torture, punishment, and the old "let them have what they deserve."

Politicians on the right and the left seem eager to be part of something called Welfare Reform. This is "our" time to pay back all the welfare moms for not realizing the American Dream. I suppose that you expect me to be merciful to those who are down on their luck, remembering how many breaks I have received—realizing that though I was not a beneficiary of affirmative action, I did benefit from the old boy network, not to mention the time and gifts of scores of coaches, teachers, and others who gave me break after break—forget it. This is not the way the world works. This parable is about the way the world works.

I doubt that welfare costs me much more than a few dollars a year in taxes. But the bank does not show mercy to me for the thousands I owe on my mortgage, so why should I show mercy to a woman with two children to support?

See? There are parables that show us something about God. But here is a parable in which we see ourselves. We have a great deal of indebtedness and not much mercy

After the bombing in Oklahoma City, there was a citywide memorial service at which Billy Graham spoke. He began by saying something like, "We are here with you to let the healing begin. We are here to show you that a nation stands beside you in your grief. We are here to forgive." I thought to myself, listening to Dr. Graham, "I'm not sure that all of us are here to forgive. Attorney General Janet Reno has not mentioned forgiveness."

Columnist Hal Crowther recently told of a couple of friends who went to a marriage counselor. While there, these quiet people were enticed into saying too much to each other. Now, their marriage is in a shambles, says Crowther, because they just cannot forgive each other for what has been said in the counseling sessions.

Is that why we are so rarely honest with one another? Better be careful what you say to even your very best of friends because, if you say the wrong thing, if you tell too much truth which results in pain, you will pay and pay. Where forgiveness is in short supply (and isn't it always?), we tiptoe about in our relationships, fearful that we will transgress, incur a debt, and then it is over.

Perhaps you were thrilled to see O. J. Simpson walk. I am sure that you were deeply grieved to watch the brothers Menendez finally go to jail for dusting their mom and dad with a shotgun and reload. But I was not. After all, dues must be paid. Morals must be upheld. I have my standards.

It's all over the world—high and low, in the palace with the king and down in the ghetto with the servants—debts are being collected. The Palestinian bomber is repaying the Israeli soldier. The IRA booby trapper is reciprocating the Protestant extremist. The guy who held up the convenience store clerk last night in Durham is only compensating his abusive father for twenty years of debts, with interest.

In the parable we first thought we had met a merciful king, a forgiving king. But no, by the end, in anger, the king is busy extricating the fingernails of the unmerciful servant, and we realize that there is no mercy anywhere, high or low, then or now, there or here.

See? Paul is right. All have sinned and fallen short of the glory of God (Romans 3:23). We all want vengeance, even if the Bible says that vengeance belongs only to God.

Leaving a demonstration on campus against the death penalty in North Carolina—having made our statement against state-sponsored vengeance, against the retribution of the electric chair—someone was reporting a quote made by one of our politicians in support of the death penalty she had read in the newspaper just the day before. "I'd love to see Jesse Helms fry in hell," someone said. We're not against the chair, just the people who are in it!

We have met the enemy, the unforgiving, unmerciful servants, and they are us. This is a parable about us. And what is to be done with us, unmerciful as we are, when all have sinned and fallen short?

I remind you of the one who told this story, the one who, after we had whipped him, beaten him, and nailed him to the wood, said, "Father, forgive, they don't know what they're doing." Our mercilessness makes Christ's mercy shine all the brighter.

My father-in-law was attempting to comfort a grieving family whose son had just died while committing a crime. They were in grief that their son had died, in greater grief at the way he had died and what people were saying about him. "Just remember," he said, "that when your son is judged, neither I nor anyone else in this town will be making the judgment. The judge will be Christ, the one who is the embodiment of mercy."

I remind you of the one who told this story. Jesus was the one who commanded us to forgive not seven times, but seventy-seven times. And who of us has obeyed? All have sinned and fallen short of the glory of God. Yet God's glory is that at last count, God has forgiven us about seventy times seven billion times seven.

Reflections

Peter asks, "Lord, how often shall I forgive?" Jesus answers, then he tells a story. At first, the story seems to be about a gracious, very gracious king. The astronomically high sum of ten thousand talents is a bit exaggerated, but nevertheless it underscores the extravagance of the ruler's graciousness. At first, the story seems to be about God, the most gracious of sovereigns.

Yet the story takes an ugly turn. When the once gracious king finds out about the servant's ungracious behavior with his fellow servant, the ruler's grace turns to very ugly vengeance. What do we make of that?

In interpreting this parable, we ought to be careful not to equate the king with God. Jesus does not tell us this is a story about God. Who is the sovereign who was once forgiving but quickly becomes unforgiving? I interpreted it as a story, not about the graciousness of God, but about our shocking ungraciousness. Having been forgiven of our astronomically high debts by God, we are incredibly ungracious to those who owe us.

Jesus is not only the one who urges forgiveness; Jesus is also the one who embodies forgiveness. Jesus forgives. In the light of Jesus' forgiveness, our lack of forgiveness is all the more apparent. As I read the story, what really got to me was the violence of it, the way that everyone in the story, the ruler on high and the servant down low, was in the business of violence and vengeance. The story seemed to be us all over.

Sometimes Jesus tells parables in order to say something to us. At other times Jesus tells parables in order to do something to us, to entrap us in our own deceit, to hold the harsh mirror of truth up to our faces, to give us the grace—for just one moment—to see ourselves as God sees us. I believe this parable

84

of the unforgiving servant or, as I might call it, the story of the forgiving then unforgiving king lures us into the story then uses it to reveal to us our own caughtness in the web of vengeance and retribution and, therefore, our need for salvation.

Speaking on the Duke campus recently, Houston Smith, a great scholar of world religions, was asked to comment on the uniqueness of Christianity as a religion. His reply: the Christian stress upon forgiveness as the way of God. No other faith, according to Smith, places forgiveness as the central attribute of God and as the central requirement of those who love God.

The parable stresses how we are caught in a web of vengeance and retribution. Yet the one who tells the parable, the one who holds the harsh mirror of truth up to our faces, is also the one who looked down from the cross as we crucified him and prayed, "Father, forgive them."

Only those words enable us to tell a different story of our lives together.

Arthritis of the Spirit

Barbara Brown Taylor

Then Peter came and said to him, "Lord, if another member of the church sins against me, how often should I forgive? As many as seven times?" Jesus said to him, "Not seven times, but, I tell you, seventy-seven times." (Matthew 18:21-22)

In case you have not noticed, Christianity is a religion in which the sinners have all the advantages. They can step on your feet fifty times, and you are supposed to keep smiling. They can talk bad about you every time you leave the room, and it is your job to excuse them with no thought of getting even. The burden is on you, because you have been forgiven yourself, and God expects you to do unto others as God has done unto you.

This is not a bad motivation for learning how to forgive. If God is willing to stay with me in spite of my meanness, my weakness, my stubborn self-righteousness, then who am I to hold those same things against someone else? Better I should confess my own sins than keep track of yours, only it is hard to stay focused on my shortcomings. I would so much rather stay focused on yours, especially when they are hurtful to me.

Staying angry with you is how I protect myself from you. Refusing to forgive you is not only how I punish you; it is also how I keep you from getting close enough to hurt me again. And nine times out of ten it works, only there is a serious side effect. It is called bitterness, and it can do terrible things to the human body and soul.

Recently, on a trip into Atlanta I stopped at a gift shop to buy a couple of wedding presents, some nice brass picture frames, which I asked the clerk to wrap. "Well, who are they for?" she snarled. "Are you going to tell me or am I supposed to guess?" I looked at her then for the first time and saw a heavy, middle-aged woman whose brow was all bunched up over two hard, cold eyes. Her mouth turned down at the sides as if she had just tasted something rancid, and she had both her hands planted on the glass counter, leaning against it with such malice that I thought she might push it over on me if I irritated her any further.

Generally speaking, I get mad when someone comes at me like that, but this time I just got scared, because I could see what her anger had done to her and I wanted to get away from it before it did something similar to me. Actually, it was something stronger than plain anger that had twisted that woman's face. All by itself, anger is not that damaging. It is not much more than that quick rush of adrenaline you feel when you are being threatened. It tells you that something you hold dear is in danger—your property, your beliefs, your physical safety. I think of anger as a kind of flashing yellow light. "Caution," it says, "something is going on here. Slow down and see if you can figure out what it is."

When I do slow down, I can usually learn something from my anger, and if I am lucky I can use the energy of it to push for change in myself or in my relationships with others. Often I can see my own part in what I am angry about, and that helps, because if I had a hand in it then I can concentrate on getting my hand back out of it again instead of spinning my wheels in blame. I can, in other words, figure out what my anger has to teach me and then let it go. But when my anger goes on and on without my learning or changing anything, then it is not plain anger anymore. It has become bitterness instead. It has become resentment, which a friend of mine calls "arthritis of the spirit."

So there is another motivation for learning how to forgive—not only because we owe it to God but because we owe it to ourselves. Because resentment deforms us. Because unforgiveness is a boomerang. We use it to protect ourselves—to hurt back before we can be hurt again—but it has a sinister way of circling right back at us so that we become the victims of our own ill will.

One summer the *New York Times Book Review* ran a series on the deadly sins. Joyce Carol Oates wrote on despair, Gore Vidal wrote on pride, and John Updike, of all people, wrote on lust. Mary Gordon's essay on anger was a real beauty, chiefly because she was willing to admit she knew a lot about it. One hot August afternoon, she wrote, she was in the kitchen preparing dinner for ten. Although the house was full of people, no one offered to help her chop, stir, or set the table. She was stewing in her own juices, she said, when her seventy-eight-year-old mother and her two small children insisted that she stop what she was doing and take them swimming.

They positioned themselves in the car, she said, leaning on the horn and shouting her name out the window so all the neighbors could hear them, loudly reminding her that she had promised to take them to the pond. That, Gordon said, was when she lost it. She flew outside and jumped on the hood of the car. She pounded on the windshield. She told her mother and her children that she was never, ever going to take any of them anywhere and none of them was ever going to have one friend in any house of hers until the hour of their death—which, she said, she hoped was soon.

Then the frightening thing happened. "I became a huge bird," she said. "A carrion crow. My legs became hard stalks, my eyes were sharp and vicious. I developed a murderous beak. Greasy black feathers took the place of arms. I flapped and flapped. I blotted out the sun's light with my flapping." Even after she had been forced off the hood of the car, she said, it took her a while to come back to herself and when she did she was appalled, because she realized she had genuinely frightened her children. Her son said to her, "I was scared because I didn't know who you were."

"Sin makes the sinner unrecognizable," Gordon concluded, and the only antidote to it is forgiveness, but the problem is that anger is so exciting, so enlivening, that forgiveness can seem like a limp surrender. If you have ever cherished a resentment, you know how right it can make you feel to have someone in the world whom you believe is all wrong. You may not be up to admitting it yet, but one of the great benefits of having an enemy is that you get to look good by comparison. It also helps to have someone to blame for why your life is not turning out the way it was supposed to.

Not long ago on National Public Radio I heard Linda Wirtheimer talking to a correspondent in the Middle East about the amazing things that are happening there between Israelis and Palestinians. "How are people reacting?" she asked him. "After all, losing an enemy is as upsetting as losing a friend." I hadn't thought about it that way before, but she is right. When you allow your enemy to stop being your enemy, all the rules change. Nobody knows how to act any more, because forgiveness is an act of transformation. It does not offer the adrenaline rush of anger, nor the feeling of power that comes from a well-established resentment. It is a quiet revolution, as easy to miss as a fist uncurling to become an open hand, but it changes people in ways that anger only wishes it could.

So why don't we do it more often? Because it is scary to lay down your arms like that, to trade in your pride and your power on the off-chance that you may discover something more valuable than either of them. "To forgive," writes Mary Gordon, "is to give up the exhilaration of one's own unassailable rightness." And there is loss in that, only it is the loss of an illusion, and what is gained is unmistakably real: the chance to live again, free from the bitterness that draws the sweetness from our lives, that gives us scary faces and turns us into carrion crows who blot out the sun with our flapping. No one else does this to us. We do it to ourselves, but we do not have to.

We are being forgiven every day of our lives. We are being set free by someone who has arranged things so that we have all the advantages. We have choices. We have will. And we have an advocate, who seems to know that we need lots of practice at this forgiveness business. How often should we forgive? Will seven times take care of it? "Not seven times," Jesus said, "but, I tell you, seventy-seven times." This is no chore. This is a promise, because forgiveness is the way of life. It is God's cure for the deformity our resentments cause us. It is how we discover our true shape, and every time we do it we get to be a little more alive. What God knows and we don't yet is that once we get the hang of it, seventy times seven won't be enough, not to mention seventy-seven. We'll be so carried away by it that we'll hope it never ends.

Forgiving the Unforgivable?

M. Basil Pennington

I t was a moment that will be forever etched in my memory. I was in the airport in Wichita waiting to board my plane when the news was flashed on the TV screens: Sadat had been shot. It was not yet known how seriously he had been injured. When I boarded my plane, I found myself seated next to a man from Kuwait, dressed in the traditional garb of his country. We began to speak together very amicably, sharing the different spiritual practices of our particular traditions. After we had been talking for about a half hour, I expressed the concern that was gripping my heart, "Isn't it tragic about Sadat?" My friend's response shocked me, "I thank Allah for wiping that curse from the face of the earth." In my shock I blurted out, "What about peace?" His response shocked me even more, "Peace is no concern of ours." Up to that time I had lived with the prejudice or "listening" that everyone wanted peace. The painful awakening of that moment put a lot of things into a new perspective.

My time in East Africa was another such awakening experience. I judge my weeks in East Africa to have been among the most painful of my life. One nun summed up the situation this way, "I speak of the three Ds: drought, darkness, and death." Drought is bad enough—in some places it is deadly, in others it inflicts incalculable sufferings, great and small. The lack of electricity certainly has a profound effect on life. When it becomes difficult to do anything from sunset to sunrise, one senses a great curtailment of life.

But it was the prevalence of death and violence that most affected me. There are long prevailing tribal animosities, which the Christian spirit often seems to fail to heal. Added to these is the pandemic plague of AIDS. The sisters working among the people said that 35 percent of the people have it, and up to 50 percent of these people live in the slums. There is virtually no medical care for the victims. What little medical expertise and supplies are available are used to treat malaria and other curable diseases. A very high unemployment rate leads hoards of hopeless AIDS victims to form bands or join guerrilla groups which sweep down upon villages, rape the women, steal all the supplies they can find, and set fire to what remains.

In front of our monastery at Butende, Uganda, there is a solitary grave that remains a gruesome reminder for all the nuns within. Sister Agnes was hacked to death as she held off a band that had broken through the convent wall. Her bravery enabled her sisters to escape into the forest. The monastery of Clarte Dieu in Zaire has been repeatedly taken by bands of brigands. After the last raid, the government caught five of the raiders and wanted—to the horror of the nuns—to hang the men at the gate of the monastery. Two days after I arrived a guerrilla band from the hills in the west swept down on a college, locked 80 students in the dormitories, and burned them alive, taking 120 others with them as hostages. Two days before I left, an armed band from the north, calling itself the Army of the Lord, seized a girls' college and took 157 of the young women to be sex slaves.

Immersed in this horror, I was confronted for the first time with the question: Are some sins unforgivable? Can a woman, a nun, a consecrated virgin, who is raped and left with AIDS and a child in her womb forgive? Can a father who has been forced to watch his wife and daughters be raped and brutalized forgive? When it is allowed to happen again and again? Are there unforgivable sins?

I believe in the power of the resurrection. The first gift of the Risen Lord was the power of forgiveness and the peace it is to bring. "Peace be with you. Whose sins you shall forgive, they are forgiven them." The Catholic Church has tended to give this moment a hierarchical interpretation. Here was conferred the bishops' and priests' power to forgive in the Sacrament of Reconciliation.

Jesus certainly knew our need to unburden ourselves and to

hear the word of forgiveness. Many psychologists have said to me as a priest that they wished they could speak this authoritative word of divine forgiveness.

There is power in the sacrament: power to believe ("Lord, I believe, help my unbelief"); power to accept forgiveness; power to forgive one's self. But I believe that a nonhierarchical interpretation of this text is also supremely important. When we forgive, any of us, God forgives. Remember the woman taken in adultery (where was the man?): "Has no one condemned you? . . . Neither do I condemn you. Go your way, and from now on do not sin again" (John 8:10-11). This also takes place at home and with others. When we truly forgive ourselves, we open the space for divine forgiveness.

When the apostles asked Jesus to teach them how to pray, he responded with a prayer that is an entire school of prayer, an entire school of life. It is awesome. And it is frightening. Forgive us our trespasses as we forgive those who trespass against us. I have always hastened to add in my heart, "Lord, I forgive everyone as fully as I can."

What would that statement mean if I had been a victim of violent abuse, of rape? Could I really forgive? By myself, I am certain I could not. As I smarted under such a humiliation and degradation of my human dignity and watched my life being sucked away by an uncontrollable virus, I would not be able to stand in the place of forgiveness and reconciliation. It would be beyond the human. There are unforgivable sins.

But in the power of the Risen Christ? I can do all things in Christ who strengthens me. As long as I retained enough of my humanity to make an act of the will, I could by God's grace cut through all and say, "I forgive." This, of course, would not immediately heal all the feelings and emotions stored, physically and mentally, in my memory. Some of this residue may never be healed in this life's journey. I would have to repeatedly cut through the remnants with acts of forgiveness. This forgiving would itself begin the process of healing. Meditation, centering prayer, would—little by little—continue the process. Others can receive the healing of my forgiveness only if they are willing to repent and accept forgiveness. The same is true of myself. I have to forgive myself of real and imagined failures.

Part of my forgiveness of others is to pray for them, pray that they receive the grace to repent and be converted. And even as I do this, my own heart is healed. That beautiful human sentiment of compassion begins to grow within me. If I am able to get some distance from my own horrible pain and grief through such prayer, I can begin to realize that the person is the sinner that he or she is as a result of having been sinned against and is very much a victim as well.

Accepting the power to forgive from Christ is more important to me than it is to the person whom I forgive. It alone opens the way to healing for self, for the other, for society.

There are indeed unforgivable sins. It is only by the infinite mercy of a God who went so far as to sacrifice God's own son, that we can forgive them and that they can be forgiven. The forgiveness that I found among the monks and nuns in East Africa is indeed a powerful witness to the resurrection and the continuing power of the Risen Christ in our midst.

Forgiveness with Justice

Margaret Hebblethwaite

Y ou can say, if they come to kill me that I forgive and bless those who do it." With these words, spoken to a journalist two weeks before his murder, Archbishop Oscar Romero forgave his assassins not only before they repented but even before they committed their crime. Is this a model of Christian forgiveness? Does it make sense?

The great majority of parents whose children have been murdered say not only that they have not forgiven but that they do not want to forgive. Indeed, they think it would be wrong to forgive. To forgive, they feel, would be to minimize the crime and would be a cruel insult to their dead child. It is too trite to dismiss this objection out of hand, for there is a great deal in it that must be taken seriously. These parents have had an experience that most of us have not had. They have first-hand knowledge where most of us can only pontificate from afar.

And there is more to it than that. The notion of forgiveness has become cheapened, and in the most common usage of the term, these parents have a point. If forgiving means what usually is meant when that word is used, then the parents should not forgive the murderers—to do so would indeed devalue their children's lives. No value can be placed on a human life. The loved one is unique and incomparable, and her or his life is priceless, irreplaceable, and worthy of a grief that is unending and inconsolable.

Usually when we say "I forgive you," it is said lightly and as an alternative way of saying "it's all right" or "it doesn't matter." But when a life has been taken, it would be deeply wrong to say "it's all right." Saying "it doesn't matter" would be outrageous and appalling. This is the point made by the "unforgiving" bereaved parents: they are saying they will not demean themselves in such a way.

The trouble with forgiveness talk (as it is commonly used) is that it is used too lightly, so that it minimizes sin and ignores the need for making amends. When faced with an irreversible situation—a dead body or a maimed one—it has nothing to offer.

"You have blinded my eyes, blown off my right hand, put me in a wheelchair, and condemned me to a lifetime of pain. But it's all right, it doesn't matter." To say that would be absurd. It would show a ludicrous sense of unreality. To say it on behalf of other people, who are no longer alive to speak for themselves, would be not only mad but very wrong indeed.

What is needed, then, is a kind of forgiveness that is able to say, "It *does* matter terribly. It will never be all right. But still I forgive you." To say this is to tap into the depths of the Christian notion of forgiveness. True forgiveness is not the excusing of sin but a force powerful enough to meet sin head-on, count the cost of it, and overturn it.

The deeply unfashionable notion of "satisfaction" is the missing link that restores forgiveness to its true strength. Traditional theology said that what the death of Christ did for us on Calvary was to make satisfaction. It was an essential factor in the Anselmian notion of how the atonement works: sin offends against the natural order and against the infinite goodness of God in a way so terrible that only the sacrifice of an innocent and infinitely valuable victim can make up for it.

Many Christians, and most feminists, have reacted against this notion, maintaining that it presents God as a heartless tyrant who would brutally sacrifice God's own child to balance some metaphysical mathematical formula. But it is time to listen again to the old wisdom. When faced with an appalling sin nothing can make up for—not thirty years in jail, not even the execution of the offender—there is more to be said than "it's all right; it doesn't matter."

What the notion of satisfaction does is to give reassurance that God can do something to put the worst things right again. Thus there is no criminal so depraved that she or he cannot be reconciled. Not even Myra Hindley, perhaps least of all Myra Hindley.[1] And there is no sin so great that it cannot be forgiven. Does keeping Myra Hindley in prison for the rest of her life make up for "the Moors Murders"? Of course not. Does it bring satisfaction to the bereaved parents to see their child's murderer fry in an electric chair? Of course not. As the U.S. friend of death-row prisoners, Sr. Helen Prejean, said, "It is like drinking salt water."

Yet there can be reconciliation and forgiveness after these atrocities, but only if satisfaction is made on a level that restores justice. Satisfaction must fight sin, not by minimizing its power, but by assessing every inch of its iniquity and putting in the balance a goodness that is even more powerful and more weighty. Only an infinite goodness will be enough for that.

Forgiveness is more than turning the other cheek—not that turning the other cheek is not commendable and often necessary, but forgiveness is on another plane altogether. True Christian forgiveness is a way of showing just how appalling sin is, because the ultimate message of forgiveness is this:

> What you have done is so terrible that nothing like that must ever be allowed to happen again on this earth. Every fiber of my being and every ounce of my energy must be turned to fighting this evil. To put a stop to such things happening I will break the cycle. Instead of repaying injury with injury, hurt with hurt, I will put a spoke in the wheel of revenge and stop it dead in its path. The cycle is broken.

Forgiving, then, is a solemn act of great power. It fights violence not with weakness but with a strength against which sin becomes useless and enfeebled. Forgiveness is not the excusing of evil, but an accusation that is also a remission. It says, "You have sinned; you have gravely sinned," but there is no split-second pause between saying that and adding, "And I waive my right of retribution."

97

Let me give another example of true forgiveness exerting its power. Luis Perez Aguirre is a Uruguayan Jesuit who lives in a community that rescues street children and brings them up in an extended, adoptive family. He is also a worker for human rights, and during the violent spell of military dictatorship in his country from 1973 to 1985, he was detained and tortured several times. On one of these occasions the torture was so bad that his tormenter took off Luis' blindfold for the perverted pleasure of eye contact between torturer and victim. It is often said there is no relationship more intimate than that, as you come to know all of the responses of the other.

There, experiencing the most appalling agonies endured by any human being and before he lost consciousness, Luis told his torturer that he would never inflict such pain upon him or upon his family and that if he came out alive he would pardon him. And he looked him in the face. A few years later, after the regime was overthrown, Luis saw the man in the street, some fifty yards away. The torturer tried to cross the road to avoid him, but there was too much traffic to do so. Luis was able to go up to him and to ask him kindly if he was well and if his family was well. After some embarrassed formal replies the torturer escaped Luis' gentleness and complete absence of recrimination and hurried off, pleading that he was in a rush.

Just those few words, Luis felt, were worthwhile, because they were a step toward healing. They gave the torturer an opportunity to see that he was forgiven in a way that did not minimize the offense (his embarrassment was proof enough of the gravity of the past) but would enable him to face up to what he had done (because reconciliation was not impossible) and to change for the future (because he would not have to maintain his old attitudes).

Punishment in any society has three functions: deterrence, prevention, and retribution. Imprisonment deters future offenders. It protects innocent people, at least for a time, from dangerous criminals who can be controlled only by being locked up. And it shows the disgust of society toward crime, which is the merit of retribution. A world that did not flicker with horror at the concentration camps or the premeditated rape and murder of innocent children would not be civilized. Worse than that, it would not be moral. Every society needs to find a way of enabling all decent, principled people to stand together in an invincible wall of condemnation against the darkness of evil—by showing that there is no impunity for crime.

Retribution must remain at a token level, because when a life has been taken or otherwise irreparably ruined, there is no sufficient retribution—other than in the message of the Cross. Not even the execution of the criminal is sufficient—and we play God if we try to pretend that such means can put things right.

But there must be no impunity. Impunity gives a message that evil does not matter. Evil must be exposed and condemned, though it can then be forgiven. There can be amnesty after investigation in front of a truth commission, as in South Africa, if the truth is told in full and if repentance is expressed. The South African system is far from perfect, but it is the best we have found so far.

We have long given up the amputation of hands or public whipping or standing in stocks as our means of condemning the evil of sin. Capital punishment has been rightly rejected by the recent Catechism of the Catholic Church; it is almost impossible to conceive of circumstances in today's world when the death penalty could be justified, says the Catechism. It could only be permitted "if this is the only possible way of effectively defending human lives against the unjust aggressor." In other words, it could only be permitted if secure imprisonment were not possible—as has sometimes been the case for communities on the march. The Catechism explains:

> Today, in fact, as a consequence of the possibilities which the state has for effectively preventing crime, by rendering one who has committed an offence incapable of doing harm—without definitively taking away from him the possibility of redeeming himself—the cases in which the execution of the offender is an absolute necessity are very rare, if not practically non-existent.

Imprisonment is our last remaining resort for punishment of

grave crimes. Inexcusably degrading as prison conditions sometimes are, imprisonment cannot be altogether abandoned without a return to the law of the jungle.

No Christian society, however, can allow imprisonment without also allowing the release of prisoners when the requirements of deterrence and prevention have been satisfied and when a token of retribution has been made. All criminals should have the possibility, in principle, of reconciliation and reintegration, the chance to make a positive contribution to the society they have injured, though some criminals will prove in practice to be beyond reform.

They may be beyond reform, but they are not beyond forgiveness. If we say that some people are beyond forgiveness, then why not us? Since only God sees the thoughts of the hearts and can assign a true value to subjective responsibility, then how can I know that I am worthy of forgiveness when Myra Hindley or Adolf Hitler is not? Luis Perez Aguirre tells us we should never judge another through an experience he had when he was tortured and took off his blindfold to see the guard at the door standing there with tears of compassion running down his face.

If we are prepared to brand anyone else as beyond forgiveness, then we run the risk of condemning our own selves to hell. And the risk is a very big one, particularly when we know the unambiguous teaching of Jesus, "if you forgive others their trespasses, your heavenly Father will also forgive you; but if you do not forgive others, neither will your Father forgive your trespasses" (Matthew 6:14-15).

It is easy to say the Lord's Prayer when we have nothing much to forgive. But when we are deeply sinned against, in a way that can never be righted, we learn how narrow the gate that leads to life is. It is hard to forgive then and difficult to avoid condemning ourselves by our willful refusal to accept the terms of mutual forgiveness.

But can we forgive those who are not sorry? We can offer forgiveness, but unless it is received and accepted—which implies an acknowledgment that there is a sin to forgive—it never turns into reconciliation (the new name that Catholics use for the sacrament of confession). The forgiveness of those who do not

100

repent then remains no more than an offer, an unrealized potential. Nonetheless, in practice, we know it is hard for anyone to admit that they have sinned unless the offer of forgiveness is already there. We can see that in our own relationship with God. Catholics who go to confession often find that the contrition that was so hard to squeeze out before they entered the confessional, flows freely after they have come out and are already tasting the sweetness of God's pardon. Forgiveness breaks down our internal barriers of resistance to admitting we were at fault. It calls forth the ability to see sin for what it is and reject it.

Forgiveness, then, is no simple, quick transaction with one person saying "sorry" and the other replying with a pardon. The transaction is an ongoing process: a preliminary gesture of forgiveness calls forth an apology, which in turn calls forth a more full-hearted and unrestrained forgiveness.

Reconciliation is an ongoing relationship in which healing becomes deeper as it becomes mutual. Forgiveness is itself transformed from a difficult act of the will in obedience to God to a warmth of reconciliation that is its final fruit. Natural justice is not outraged by the transaction but reaffirmed.

This, of course, means there must be a firm purpose of amendment. To accept forgiveness without putting things right for the future is a deceitful game. In South Africa the whites' acceptance of the forgiveness from the blacks means that they are willing to reform the imbalances of economic power. That is not an extra, optional step: it is part of the very core of the transaction of reconciliation.

Likewise, in Northern Ireland the Protestants' acceptance of the forgiveness of the Catholics means that they are willing to reform the imbalances of power. And by accepting the forgiveness of the Protestants the Catholics show that they are willing to lay aside forever not only the weapons of violence but also the weapons of past resentment.

While the offer of forgiveness may be made on one side only, reconciliation is an ongoing commitment on both sides to a changed and ever-changing relationship. The "theology of reconciliation" has been given a bad name in some Latin American countries where it has been used to mean impunity without confession, without repentance, and without change. This misuse of reconciliation makes a travesty of Christian teaching.

The usual form of the Lord's Prayer says, "forgive us our trespasses, as we forgive those who trespass against us." But the Gospels use a different word: "debts." A more accurate translation is, "forgive us our debts, as we also have forgiven our debtors." This used to sound inadequate and rather quaint for sin, but in today's world we begin to see the point.

Debt has become a huge issue of international ethics. Honduras and Nicaragua were both on their knees even before Hurricane Mitch. Between them, they were paying more than $2 million every day in debt charges. The evil of exacting these crucifying payments turned into a farce after the hurricane, when well-meaning contributors responded to appeals for funds, and found that whatever money they were able to raise was no more than a crumb to feed the gaping jaws of the creditors.

The blinding number of naughts on the end of these sums inoculate us to the reality of what is at issue: debt for the Third World equals thousands, if not millions, of human lives. This is the true mortal sin, the sin that kills.

"Break the chains of debt" was the slogan of the Jubilee 2000 campaign when it went to Birmingham, England, in May 1998 to demand release for the debtor nations. Break the chains of debt is the cry we should utter every time we forgive. As a forceful act, forgiveness has the strength to break chains. The bigger the chains, the more powerful are the words of the one who says "I forgive you."

The one who forgives takes the order of justice in hand and spins it around to correct its direction. The world, which had begun to hurtle off course, is restored to its true dynamic. Whereas injury calls forth injury and hate calls forth hate, kindness calls forth kindness and love calls forth love. That is a fact, and it can be easily observed.

To draw a line beneath all the hurting that has gone on in the world and say "no more" is the way to bring about the rule of God that Isaiah speaks of so movingly:

The wolf shall live with the lamb,
  the leopard shall lie down with the kid, . . .
They will not hurt or destroy
  on all my holy mountain;
for the earth will be full of the knowledge of the LORD
  as the waters cover the sea. (Isaiah 11:6-9)

Note

1. Myra Hindley has served more than thirty years in prison in England for helping her lover torture and kill several young children in what came to be called "the Moors Murders."

The Process of Forgiveness

Joseph Coyne

I n the 1960s the phrase "Think globally while acting locally" was often used by the ecology movement to keep people from becoming paralyzed in their efforts to save the
world because of the enormousness of the task. In effect,
the slogan conveyed the idea that if we simply take better care
of our neighborhoods, the world will eventually be a better
place.

This same philosophy may be of help when considering the
issue of forgiveness. Forgiveness can have global dimensions.
How does one address the issue of forgiving men like Adolf
Hitler or Pol Pot who committed crimes of such magnitude?
Their acts paralyze the mind; talking about forgiveness to peo-
ple who have been injured by such men seems beyond words.

Forgiveness can have local and international dimensions
when considering how groups of people such as the Israelis and
the Palestinians, or the Serbs and their neighbors, can learn to
forgive each other and live in peace. On a global level, the issue
of forgiveness can take on such complexity that addressing it
paralyzes the mind. Perhaps addressing the issue of forgiveness
locally, by looking at the difficulty one person may have forgiving another, could in a small way begin to free the mind. Is it
possible that when we begin to take better care of our own
neighborhood, we contribute to building a better world?

It is likely that the problem of forgiveness has been important
in our spiritual and interpersonal lives since our ancestors first
banded together for survival. Forgiveness is a central theme in
the Bible, which fundamentally relates the story of humankind's
six-thousand-year journey with God. In the most ancient books

of the Bible, forgiveness may have been directed primarily toward the members of the tribe (that is, the followers of Yahweh), but with the passage of time the issue of forgiveness has broadened. Matthew's Gospel tells the story of Peter's struggle with forgiveness when he asked Jesus how often he should forgive his brother "if he asks for forgiveness." No doubt Peter felt he was being quite generous when he suggested to Jesus that he should perhaps forgive his brother as many as seven times. As we all know, Jesus used this as a "growth opportunity" for Peter when he advised him that "seventy-seven times" would be more like it!

The proliferation of forgiveness imperatives has not stopped during the last two thousand years. Recently I typed the word "forgiveness" into my Internet search engine, and in less that thirty seconds found well over thirty-five thousand hits. A cursory look at a random sample of them revealed that the vast majority were religious references, listing innumerable scriptural and theological instructions to forgive our brothers and sisters. There appears to be a lot of advice concerning the benefits of forgiveness, both spiritual and emotional, but little information on how to achieve it. Even Jesus' response to Peter leaves this aspect of the subject unaddressed, since the question asked only how many times you should forgive *if* your brother asks for it.

In my work as both a priest and a psychotherapist, it has been my experience that most people are able to forgive (given some time), if their transgressor is sincerely sorry for his or her actions. The vexing problem for most of the people I work with is how to forgive someone who has not asked to be forgiven. In fact, many times transgressors not only omit the expression of regret, they may be lacking regret altogether.

Trudy Grover, in her article "The Ethics of Forgiveness," makes the point that forgiveness happens when three elements are present: the victim, the offender, and the mutual understanding that the victim has been wronged. She strongly implies that if the offender is unwilling to acknowledge wrongdoing, then forgiveness will remain unattainable and, to the victim, will seem more like moral excuses than a serious attempt at reconciliation. Grover also observes, however, that people who are willing to forgive when their offender admits culpability often enhance their emotional health. This supports the lesson Jesus taught Peter but adds one further dimension; namely, if the offender fails to admit having done something wrong, forgiveness may not be possible.

Still the question remains: can one forgive in the absence of regret and an admission of wrongdoing? Will life exact a price for our failure to achieve a measure of forgiveness toward those who have hurt us but refuse to ask for forgiveness?

I still remember a chance meeting nearly fifteen years ago with the mother of one of my students. Her story, while not unique, impressed me since she was in the end stages of her battle with lung cancer. She had experienced a very painful divorce fifteen years earlier, and by her telling, she had spent all of those years hating her former husband for abandoning her. Her former spouse, apparently, felt no regret at all. He had remarried soon after the divorce and, by all accounts, was living a reasonably happy life. On one of our last visits together, she shared with me an insight learned from her illness, "Father, I wasted the last fifteen years of my life hating that bastard. Boy, I wish I had those years back now!"

It is clear that the inability to forgive can cost us dearly. In working with my psychotherapy clients, I have observed time and again that progress really begins when the process of forgiveness is underway. Yet the question remains about what spiritual or psychological process allows us to forgive those who have hurt us. Must those of us who have been severely injured by "unrepentant" others wait until our deathbeds to gain the motivation required to move on in life just as we prepare to move out of it?

In response to this dilemma, some maintain that forgiveness is primarily an act of the will and, therefore, should not be confused with any emotional change in attitude. In this view, forgiveness begins with a conscious decision to let go of the hurt and anger by deciding we want to forgive. This decision is then followed by a change in attitude. In my work, however, I have known people who really wanted to achieve a measure of forgiveness in their lives, but seemed unable to do so. If forgiveness is simply an act of the will, this result is hard to explain. The reason for this difficulty, I believe, lies not in our heads but rather in our hearts.

The emotion most often associated with the kind of painful experiences we are talking about is anger. In a very real sense then, deciding to forgive means dealing with our anger. Raymond DiGiuseppe has researched and written much about the difficulties associated with anger and its management. He has found that as an emotion, anger is relatively frequent in both males and females and tends to last longer than most other affective states. Anger also tends to provoke more verbal expression than other emotions do, and it evokes the strongest changes in our voice. Perhaps most interesting, however, is DiGiuseppe's assertion that people usually feel little desire to change or control their experience of anger. In fact, the only other emotion people are less likely to want to change is joy. As a result of his work, DiGiuseppe views anger as not simply an internal feeling state, but as a condition that involves the mind and the body, arousing us in ways that make it difficult for us to leave the experience. It appears that anger produces a strong pull in us, drawing us to approach it rather than avoid its root cause.

While this may be difficult to accept, my work has often reinforced this insight. Recently this phenomenon surrounding anger took one of the student interns I supervise completely by surprise. In his defense, most beginning clinicians do not deal well with anger and often find that ignoring anger is preferable to dealing with it. Occasionally, however, a client will have none of that, and this young clinician rapidly realized that his was such a client. She had recently experienced a painful divorce, and during their sessions she repeatedly relived her experience of being rejected by her spouse. With each passing week, her anger grew more intense in the sessions, and the therapist eventually found himself the target of many of these angry attacks. The client would repeatedly accost him for not really helping her, challenging him to do something for her. After several weeks the therapist began to express concern about his physical safety, even though no overt acts or threats were made. We worked on ways to deal with the situation, but none seemed effective. In the end, feeling quite helpless and defeated, the intern felt it best to relinquish the case.

During my first session, I pointed out to the client that her anger was hindering her progress. Her response was a rather mystified expression, followed by the comment, "What do you mean? Everybody has been telling me that I should express my anger and get it out in therapy! How can that be hindering my progress? I thought that was progress." While that might be good advice for some people, she was quite good at "doing anger." In fact, anger was the one emotion she did very well! What she was failing to see was that expressing her anger only bred more anger, which in the end tended to scare people away. This in turn only intensified her sense of abandonment, which then increased her depression. Finally, once she was feeling really depressed and isolated, she tended to become even more angry, hated her former husband even more, and so on. My advice to this young woman was, simply put, "Don't go there! When you are at home and your anger begins to well up inside, realize it doesn't do you any good. In your therapy, don't attempt to get in touch with your anger and hurt, you can do a fine job of that on your own. Use your sessions to learn how to deal with those feelings, and in the end, you will not want to go there!"

Much emotional and spiritual growth really involves developing the capacity to "not go there" in regard to our anger, but to do something else with it. While this may seem childishly simple, developing this ability, which is the capacity to forgive and move on in life, is quite challenging. In working with individuals who are in the midst of this struggle, I am always impressed by how vivid the memories of painful events remain. While years may have elapsed, the recollections of others' past transgressions can fill the therapy room as if they had happened yesterday. In his work, DiGiuseppe has observed that angry memories often draw us ever deeper into the effect they produce. This can actually make our anger and hurt deeper and more pervasive. In the end, that which began as an event, can come to define who we are as a person. In psychological terms, a state can become a lifelong trait, or an event that caused us to become angry, if brooded over long enough, can come to express who we are as a person.

As in the case with the young woman whose husband recently left her, the factor common to most of these experiences is the perception of an injustice, coupled with the belief that someone else is at fault. Such events often challenge our self-esteem. The issue of forgiving raises the question, "How could that person have done this to me?" It is coupled with the belief, "I have never done anything to deserve this; I never act like this toward others!" The anger we feel is often fueled by both of these assumptions. Working to forgive, then, involves struggling with a sense of injustice and the belief that we ourselves are blameless, or at least did nothing that would have justified this situation. In essence working to forgive includes struggling with the belief, "I have been wronged, and I can recall no instances where I have wronged others in a similar fashion." In my experience, if either of these two elements are absent, forgiveness is much easier. In my work as both a priest and a psychotherapist, it is those situations where the feelings of injustice and blamelessness are combined that our capacity to forgive is challenged the greatest.

I have come to believe that forgiveness is not an event, rather it is a process. In working with people who have struggled to forgive truly painful events, I have discovered that forgiveness has not been reached in a moment in time, although the realization that forgiveness has, in fact, occurred may suddenly grasp them. If asked when it happened, usually they cannot identify any specific day, time, or event. Instead, they begin to talk about feeling less angry or hurt and being more understanding of the events involved. In this sense, those who assert that forgiveness is a decision or act of the will that takes place in a moment in time may be commenting on the realization that forgiveness has taken place, but they may be ignoring the process that achieved it. The only decision most people are aware of is that they are tired of being angry and want to be free of it. This is often the point when they begin to seek help, but not the day the goal is achieved. The process they are embarking on takes time and represents a change in perspective in the end.

Reaching the goal often begins by accepting a difficult concept, namely that we are "average." Averageness is hard for most of us to accept since the messages we receive in our society tell us it is important to be unique, to stand out from the crowd.

After all, who likes to think of themselves as average? Who, for instance, wants a C in a class? Certainly not me, I am above average at least, if not outstanding. Who wants to consider himself or herself part of the crowd? We all strive to stand out from the crowd, to be unique. The call to averageness seems ridiculous; yet, I believe it is the beginning of the road we seek—if that road involves forgiving someone.

The road to forgiveness actually begins by realizing that we ourselves have acted in ways that others may have found offensive. For instance, when a driver cuts me off on the freeway and I react with anger, it is because he has no right to do that to me! I quickly think to myself, "I didn't cut him off! Look at that jerk! Who does he think he is? Man I'm glad I don't drive like that!" If at this crucial moment I can simply think, "Well, maybe at times I have driven like that," I can save myself a fifteen-point rise in blood pressure. Once I realize it is possible that I have, in fact, committed at least similar offenses when rushed or driving carelessly, the anger and injustice I feel often dissipate. Today he is the jerk; tomorrow it may well be me! With this understanding begins the realization that I may be average after all or just like everybody else.

In the process of accepting our averageness, our perception of the offending person often starts to change. Perhaps he or she is not altogether worthless and uncaring, but rather something else, something more like ourselves. When we think about some of the truly horrific acts committed in the course of human history, we usually see little of ourselves in the people who commit them. But when we look more deeply into the bigotry or hatred at the core of such actions, perhaps we can see a little of ourselves that requires some self-awareness and watching. When we are entering into the process of forgiveness, we may be entering into a process that will change our perception not only of others, but also ourselves.

In reflecting on her own process of forgiveness, a client began her account by noting, "For four years I was angry. I didn't think I was angry; I would have said 'hurt.'" The incident that had occupied so much of her energy and time over the last four years occurred at a family reunion which she had been instrumental in setting up. She had gotten a beach house for herself and her sisters, but the event had been transformed from the small gathering she intended into a large gathering of more than twenty-two siblings, spouses, and friends. Having lived alone since the death of her husband, she felt increasingly more overwhelmed by the size of the crowd as the weekend progressed, until she knew she had to get away for a while to save her sanity. Upon her return, she was greeted with a cool detachment that eventually ended in a family confrontation.

After the event little was said, but a very close bond had been broken. As a result, a number of family activities that once had been harmonious now became strained. Holidays were shortened and sister reunions were skipped. Of this period she wrote:

> I just didn't stay around too long, maybe 3 or 4 hours at the longest, never overnight. Then gradually I spent time alone with each sister and even spent a night in each one's home. Through all of this I realized I did love them. And I thought I had forgiven them because I didn't wish them any harm. But none of us ever referred to the incident. I know they felt badly, but I was truly scared to bring up the subject. I thought I would make a fool of myself, and I thought they would tell me how wrong I was. I couldn't face that humiliation.

She explained that every time she thought of the incident, she would go over what they had said and what she had said, and she would always feel she was in the right—at least far more than they. After all, who got the house in the first place? "I don't even like the beach, yet I 'sacrificed' a whole week and flew down there just so they could enjoy this house on the bay. . . . I remembered thinking, it served them right. Let them go and, hopefully, feel guilty about my not being there."

Over the course of the four years, while H worked on a number of issues, she often returned to this issue with her family. She noted: "During all this time I talked and talked and talked in my therapy sessions about my anger with them. I remember thinking that if I wrote them a letter and took some of the blame (a very little part as I recall) maybe things would be as before." Finally during the last year of her therapy, H began to feel comfortable enough to go to family parties again without, as she noted, "dragging a friend along." H continued, "I talked a little more intimately with my sisters on the phone when I saw them." With the exception of sister reunions, everything seemed pretty normal. "We laughed and teased each other and shared some of our deepest feelings. We confided in each other once again."

While in therapy H had also begun to develop the discipline of Centering Prayer. Typically she would engage in two periods of prayer a day, during which she would attempt to empty her mind of thoughts, but she would constantly feel bombarded with remembrances that made her angry. Feeling frustrated and defeated in her attempts to curb her anger and forgive her sisters, H wrote:

> After telling my therapist that I was giving up Centering Prayer, I stated that I thought it was time I explained to my sisters why I didn't feel comfortable joining them at sister reunions. I would tell them that I did not think we had as much in common as we used to. Now that I was widowed, I was the only one who was single and I also was the only childless one. And then it dawned on me that the reason they thought I talked about myself all the time was that I did—I had no husband or children to talk about and so my sharing was about things that only interested me personally. And I probably did get a glazed look on my face when they talked about their children because of being childless. I couldn't relate to what they were saying. And then I stopped and was stunned. All my anger had dissolved. I hadn't even noticed when it left me. When I think back I wonder why I never saw things more clearly from my sisters' perspective. Why was I so hurt, that I couldn't see? When I look at it now, I think of course they felt this way and I felt that way.

Christian teaching is clear that we are all called to forgive our trespassers, but it says little about the process by which we are to achieve that goal. Often, we know what we should be striving for, so we attempt to forgive without realizing that it is only the process of working through our anger that can bring it about. H's story illustrates the process from which forgiveness emerges. For years, she experienced anger when memories of the event that produced it were lived over in her mind. She refrained from talking about it with her sisters for fear that she would only be hurt again. Since they had failed to understand her the first time, what hope was there for understanding to be achieved now, after years had passed?

While the predominant feeling H experienced was anger, anger is often a secondary emotion. In this sense, anger is often experienced in relation to another, preceding feeling. Often, when clients are attempting to understand their anger, I advise them to see if they can identify the feeling that they experienced just before they felt angry. In H's case, she clearly identified a more primary feeling when she wrote, "I felt too vulnerable being with them on my own. I feared they would strike out at me again." While most people are aware of struggling with their feelings of anger when it comes to trying to forgive, they are often unable to recognize the emotions that underlie their anger, namely vulnerability and fear. In many clients' cases, it is the feelings of vulnerability and fear that give rise to anger that make forgiveness so difficult a task.

In H's case, the process of forgiveness began by struggling with her anger, but the feelings of fear and vulnerability that had preceded it took longer to recognize. She defended herself against these emotions by feeling angry. From anger came the belief that H was not like her sisters, but rather quite different. This belief allowed her to distance herself from them with little regret. What she was distancing herself from was her feelings of fear and vulnerability. Through her therapy and spiritual practice, H developed the capacity to deal with these feelings, and with this ability came the dissipation of anger and the birth of a new perspective. This change of perspective is often so subtle an event that many people, like H, simply say, "All my anger had dissolved. I hadn't even noticed when it left me."

In describing this process, persons suddenly seem to realize they are no longer angry. This may explain why countless writers have spoken of forgiveness as an act of the will, describing it as something that seems to take place at a moment in time. But this view misses the profound change of perspective which H and others experience in the process. If we believe we must rapidly reach the end of this process by forgiving our trespassers without going through the process of changing our perspective, we run the risk of forgiving in theory but not in practice. It has been said that "Christians are great at burying the hatchet; the only problem is that [the hatchet] always marks the spot!" Marking the spot involves forgiving in theory but not in practice. Forgiveness requires a profound change in perspective, and such changes do not happen quickly. Enduring and struggling with the anger, the pain, and ultimately, the feelings of fear and vulnerability are the price each of us must pay to achieve true and lasting forgiveness in our lives.

Loving and Forgiving

Eric James

M y parents were Presbyterians. When they moved ten miles out of London to Chadwell Heath in Essex just before I was born in 1925, however, there was no local Presbyterian church, so I was sent to Sunday school at a corrugated iron Methodist chapel.

I can see Miss Womack, the pianist, raising her prehensile hands and bringing them down on the piano keys. And I can hear Mrs. Hasler, the superintendent, when the hymn was over and it was time for prayers, saying, "Now close your peepers." There was silence and then she said, "There's one little boy who hasn't yet closed his peepers." No prizes for who he was. But I can still feel the flush of guilt as I remember her words. Yet I knew forgiveness then. The warmth of God's love seemed to surround and suffuse some of the hymns we sang:

> I think when I read that sweet story of old,
> When Jesus was here among men,
> How He called little children as lambs to His fold,
> I should like to have been with them then.
> I wish that His hands had been placed on my head,
> That His arms had been thrown around me,
> And that I might have seen His kind look when He said,
> "Let the little ones come unto me!"[1]

That Methodist chapel closed down, so we became members of the Church of England: St. Chad's, Chadwell Heath. When people ask me why I am in the Church of England, I often answer with complete accuracy, "Because the Methodist church closed down."

117

When I was six or seven, Mother took me along to St. Chad's one evening when the choir was practicing and said to the choirmaster that she wanted me to join the choir. He stood me next to some other probationers and got on with the practice. After a few minutes, he came over to me and put his face close to mine to hear what my voice was like. I was simply terrified and knew at once that I could never go near him—or the choir—again. But I couldn't say that to my mother. So for several weeks on practice nights, Wednesdays and Fridays, I took a book that had church anthems in it out into the streets and learned something to sing to Mother when I got back home and she asked, "What have you learnt this evening?" That side of things went well. I can still sing an anthem, "O Dayspring," which I have never heard any choir sing anywhere. But standing under a lamppost learning an anthem, riddled with guilt at the deception I was practicing—and avoiding anyone who I thought might ask me what I was doing there—was not pleasant.

The deceit was brought to a sudden end when summer holidays came, and the vicar told my mother there was no choir practice in August. Yet I had still been going out with my anthem book. "Where were you in that first week of August?" Mother asked. Tears were the only refuge.

There had been another guilt-making incident a little earlier. I saw four pennies of my brother's pocket money on top of the sideboard. (He was four years older than I.) I removed them into my pockets, one at a time, on four consecutive days. I was still in primary school. On the way there each day I passed Mays's, a corner shop that sold sweets *and* chicken feed. I thought the chicken feed was sweets, as it sat in open sacks on the floor, and it looked as though you could get quite a lot for fourpence. Mrs. Mays, however, to my astonishment, did not immediately cooperate when I asked her for "four penn'orth of that." "You ain't got no chickens, dearie," she said. I insisted I wanted "four penn'orth of that."

Alas, at the time a friend of my brother's came into the shop and told him that afternoon in school that he'd seen me buying chicken feed. By that time, one mouthful had already persuaded me that one mouthful of chicken feed was more than enough.

When I got home, Mother was waiting to ask me where I had gotten the money for the chicken feed. More tears, and I was sent up to my bedroom until my father came home. (I still don't know what the hiding that followed taught me.) I believed for quite a while that—as I was told—they had a *liar* and a *thief* in the family. But the continuing love of a loving family must have, in due course, persuaded me I was forgiven—and, as the years went by, so did the hymns and anthems I learned as a choirboy. I did not, of course, have a sophisticated theory or theology of the atonement then, but I knew that Jesus forgave me and that God was speaking through Jesus on the Cross.

I was a young man when the Second World War broke out, and I went to work at a riverside wharf on the Thames. It was in those years that I discovered I was homosexual. My first homosexual experiences happened in London during the blackout with servicemen who were on leave. This brought more guilt.

One such serviceman, *not* homosexual, was John Rowe, who was billeted at our vicarage. He had been training for ordination at Leeds University under the auspices of the Community of the Resurrection, but had decided to join the service during the war. We immediately became friends, and I have birthday and Christmas presents from him from 1939 until he died an untimely death from a heart attack in 1970. During the war, he became a captain in the Royal Marines. After the war, he was ordained, got a double first in classics at Leeds, and was, for a time, vice principal of Wells Theological College.

It was John's friendship, rather than any book, that taught me volumes about the meaning of love: human and divine. He shared with me what sacramental confession meant to him; and I made my first confession to his parish priest at St. Martin's, Sherwood, near his home in Nottingham.

Through the years of the war, I worked at the riverside wharf, which was only a few hundred yards from Southwark Cathedral, where I learned to play the organ, either at lunchtime or in the evenings—until the Cathedral was damaged by bombs, when I transferred to the organ of Guy's Hospital Chapel.

In 1944, Cuthbert Bardsley, later Bishop of Coventry, came to

Southwark Cathedral as Provost. He became a close friend—and my confessor. At the end of the war, the music at Southwark Cathedral was some of the finest in London. The young Kathleen Ferrier sang there in Bach's "St. Matthew" and "St. John" Passions. I know of no more powerful articulation of prayer for forgiveness than the alto aria, "Have Mercy, Lord, on Me," with its solo violin accompaniment in Bach's "St. Matthew" Passion.

In 1946, I began training for ordination at King's College, London. The dean of the college, Eric Abbott, was a "friend of the soul" to many, and he became one of my closest friends. He would often recommend books to me that deepened my understanding of forgiveness—not only works of theology, but novels and plays by Graham Greene, Francois Mauriac, George Bernanos, and Tennessee Williams. The novel by Helen Waddell, *Peter Abelard,* had been published in 1933, when Eric had just become Warden of Lincoln Theological College. One particular passage in it he would often quote:

[Thibault and Abelard are walking together in some woods, when they hear the cry of a rabbit caught in a trap. Abelard releases the rabbit, but it dies.]

It was that last confiding thrust that broke Abelard's heart. He looked down at the little draggled body, his mouth shaking. "Thibault," he said, "do you think there is a God at all? Whatever has come to me, I earned it. But what did this one do?"

Thibault nodded.

"I know," he said. "Only—I think God is in it too. . . ."

"In it? Do you mean that it makes [God] suffer, the way it does us?"

Again Thibault nodded.

"Then why doesn't [God] stop it?"

"I don't know," said Thibault, "Unless—"

[They talk together of Calvary.]

[Thibault says:] "That was only a piece of it—the piece that we saw—in time. Like that." He pointed to a fallen tree beside them, sawn through the middle. "That dark ring there, it goes up and down the whole length of the tree. But you only see it where it is cut across. That is what Christ's life was; the bit of God that we saw. And we think God is like that, because Christ was like that, kind, and forgiving sins and healing people. We think God is like that for ever, because it happened once with Christ. . . ."

"Then, Thibault," he said slowly, "you think that all this," he looked down at the little quiet body in his arms, "all the pain of the world, was Christ's cross?"

"God's cross," said Thibault. "And it goes on."[2]

I was ordained priest in 1952 to St. Stephen's Rochester Row in Westminster. My vicar, George Reindorp (later Bishop of Guildford and, after that, of Salisbury), was a well-known parish priest, preacher, and confessor. It was not long before I had to hear confessions for the first time—when he was away.

It was as a young priest that I had an encounter that made me think further about the sacrament of confession. I went to one of the best-known confessors in the Church of England to make my confession. What he had to say, as he counseled me after confession, made it clear to me that he had what I could only regard as a seriously flawed understanding of homosexuality—in spite of his reputation—and was using threats to direct my exercise of what I regarded as God's gift to me: my particular sexuality. I never went to him again, but I realized that although the unworthiness of the minister does not affect the sacrament—that is to say, the absolution ministered by the priest—the counsel given in the context of the sacrament can have seriously deleterious effects. It became clear to me just how necessary it is for priests who hear confessions—sacramental or otherwise—to be trained in a true psychology, though there is no easy solution to the problem of what is a true psychology. No doubt the confessor I went to (who had books published on the work of a physician of the soul) believed his understanding of psychology to be true.

It was in 1957, in my second year as a chaplain of Trinity College, Cambridge, that I had my first book published. It was subtitled, "How to Receive Forgiveness." Its title, *The Double Cure,* was a reference to the well-known hymn, "Rock of Ages, Cleft for Me," by the eighteenth-century hymn writer August Toplady, with the lines: "Be of sin the double cure,/Cleanse me from its guilt and power."[3]

The preface I wrote to the book summed up much that I then believed about "how to receive forgiveness":

Four years in a busy central London parish as assistant-curate, and now as a chaplain of a Cambridge College of nearly a thousand members, have convinced me that everything possible must be done to proclaim that the sacrament of Confession is available for all in the Church of England.

I know so many—amongst whom I count myself—of greatly different temperaments and needs, whose lives have been transformed by the sacrament. But I know many more who need it, but are held back by some fear, lack of knowledge, or prejudice. So rarely is this sacrament mentioned in Confirmation preparation, and lasting loss is caused.

My special purpose is to proclaim that this sacrament does not belong to one part of the Church alone. It is the point at which Catholic and Evangelical meet. It mediates "Justification by Faith" in sacramental form. It is for all who need it: but many more need it than those who are aware of their need.[4]

I was much encouraged by a noted evangelical, the Reverend C. F. D. Moule, the Lady Margaret's Professor of Divinity at the University of Cambridge at the time, who wrote for the cover of the book, "Admirable. I cannot imagine a better introduction to the subject."

I did not explain in the book how it was that I came to write it. In fact, it was not intended to be a book. It was, at first, simply a talk I gave in my rooms in Trinity College. Billy Graham had recently conducted a mission to the University of Cambridge (He had eaten lunch in my rooms). He had influenced many during the mission, but I found that, one by one, a number of those at the College who had been influenced came to see me and said with dismay that although they had hoped life would be different, they were still what they were before. I said that I thought that regular sacramental confession might help them because it deals not only with the burden of momentary guilt, but also with our continuing reality.

Present at that talk in my rooms was a publisher, Leonard Cutts, who told me he wanted to turn my talk into a small book.

When it was published, it went through several editions over a period of more than twenty-five years.

Ten years later, after four years at Cambridge and several years as a parish priest in inner South London, I was the head of the reform and renewal organization Parish & People and was responsible for guiding the planning of the annual conference. We decided its subject should be "Spirituality for Today." It was a conference at which, of course, forgiveness was bound to be near the center.

There was one paper in this marvelous and seminal "sixties" conference that—not least because of what has been said previously in this essay—I considered of key importance: "Psychology and Spirituality" by Dr. Harry Guntrip of the Department of Psychiatry at Leeds University, the author of *Mental Pain and the Cure of Souls*.

I had not lost my conviction that our understanding of forgiveness must be related to a mature psychology. Already it was clear, and not only in the Anglican Church, that there was, in fact, a growing decline in the use of sacramental confession and a huge increase in the resort to the ministry of pastoral counselors and psychotherapists. Many people, it seemed to me, were in search of a more profound understanding of guilt, and thus, a more profound forgiveness. Whether they always found it where they sought it was another matter.

Dr. Guntrip's paper, centering on the work of Dr. W. R. D. Fairbairn and Dr. D. W. Winnicott, was demanding but did not disappoint us. It was, of course, not only about forgiveness but about the even larger subject of spirituality.

It was in 1972 that I was forced to face an aspect of forgiveness that I had not previously encountered personally. I had to defend someone who was a fellow member of a diocesan staff who was being unjustly attacked by those in authority over him. I could not stand aside, because I had considerable responsibility for bringing the person on to the staff. In the end, to retain my integrity, I had to move elsewhere as did the person attacked. It brought back to my mind something Eric Abbott had said to me as a student: "You are a romantic, boy, and unless you have a high doctrine of corruption, you will not survive corruption in the church as well as state." I also remembered how, during a retreat when I was a student Fr. Keble Talbot, the conductor, had said:

"The same night he was betrayed, Jesus took bread . . ." At the worst time he did the best deed. He used the betrayal for the redemption of mankind. When you are betrayed, do not add to the evil of betrayal the evil of embitterment. Use your betrayal redemptively.

That was, I learned, more easily said than done.

When I was a student, Eric Abbott introduced me to a prayer of Bishop Ken (1637–1711). It has been on my bedroom windowsill since the day of my ordination. It has needed to be there:

Give me the priest these Graces shall possess:
of an Ambassador the just Address,
A Father's Tenderness, a Shepherd's Care,
A Leader's Courage, which the Cross can bear,
A Ruler's Arm, a Watchman's wakeful Eye,
A Pilot's skills the Helm in Storms to ply,
A Fisher's Patience and a Lab'rer's Toil,
A Guide's Dexterity to disembroil,
A Prophet's Inspiration from Above,
A Teacher's Knowledge, and a Saviour's Love.
Give me the Priest, a Light upon a Hill,
Whose Rays his whole Circumference can fill;
In God's own Word, and sacred learning vers'd,
Deep in the Study of the Heart Immers'd.
Who in such Souls can the Disease descry,
And wisely fit Restoratives apply.[5]

Notes

1. *The Hymnal of the Protestant Episcopal Church in the United States of America 1940* (1961 ed.). New York: The Church Pension Fund, No. 246. Hymn by Jemima Luke.

2. Waddell, H. (1987). *Peter Abelard: A Novel*. London: Constable.

3. *Hymns and Psalms: A Methodist and Ecumenical Hymn Book* (1983).

124

London: Methodist Publishing House, No. 273. Hymn by Augustus Montague Toplady.

4. James, E. (1957). *The Double Cure: How to Receive Forgiveness*. London: Hodder and Stoughton.

5. Cropper, M. (1949). *Flame Touches Flame*. London: Longmans, Green, and Co., p. 42.

The Keys of the Kingdom

Jim Cotter

Reflecting on thirty years in ordained ministry, I recently turned to the words from the 1662 *Book of Common Prayer* of the Church of England that the Bishop of Manchester had used on a late September morning in 1968, as he and a semicircle of the "robed" (the powerful in the land?) laid hands on a young man's head. They were words of awesome power indeed. They stunned my uncle, who had known them before but never heard them uttered in such a solemn assembly—and he knew quite a bit about power as the regional sales director of a large industrial company.

"Whose sins thou dost forgive, they are forgiven, and whose sins thou dost retain, they are retained."

It is from the Gospel according to John chapter 20, verse 23, and is part of a carefully crafted story from the third generation or so of the infant churches, who were variously and slowly finding their identity in a fairly hostile world, their leaders concerned with establishing their authority and putting these terrifying words on the lips of the risen Jesus.

No, I do not believe that Jesus said these words in that context, though I do believe they can lead us to the profound truth they contain—once we have altered the perspective and changed the context. It is said that Jesus breathed on them—and forgiveness is as close as breath. It is said that the gift was the Holy Spirit—and the Holy Spirit brings each of us the gift of eternal life by bringing each of us (when we will let Her) closer to one another. It is a truth, no doubt experienced by those first followers, that is embedded deep in human relationships at all times and in all places: each of us wields the "Keys of the Kingdom" when we have power to give or withhold forgiveness. I do not believe those keys were given solely to the eleven apostles that day and, from them, to their successors, the presbyters and bishops of the churches, so that they might control the congregations in their "care"—or were the keys (and are they?) fatally mixed in with the "control" of the apostles and their successors?

Perhaps we understand these words better as a statement rather than a commission, an explicit recognition that the power to release or keep imprisoned another person is given to every human being. It expresses a profound truth about human relationships rather than one about the linchpins of a religious system.

If I offend you, admit to you my offense, and say that I am sorry and pledge that I will try not to wound you again, I put myself in your power or, as we say, at your mercy. You have a choice whether to release me from my prison, to melt the ice block in which I have been frozen. You may choose to withhold, or at least defer, that release. You can still "freeze me out." It may do neither of us any good and you may be held as much as I am, but there is little I can do if you choose to wield your power that way. You may continue for years to harbor resentment, to give it safe refuge, letting bitterness rather than compassion grow within you. Stuck fast, unable to move, at the very best our relationship will be "on hold."

There are circumstances in which your withholding will be wise. If I have "trespassed" on your territory, invaded you across a boundary that had been agreed upon, and if I do this again and again and do not recognize that I am at fault, you may well retreat into your citadel and do your best to prevent me scaling the walls again. For your safety, and with the prudence that waits for me to recognize that I have hurt you, you will, for a while, keep your distance. You may find it within you not to abandon me altogether, not to "lose touch" completely, but you will be wary. You will test me, using the time of separation to allow respect to grow again. You may even keep open a forgiving heart, waiting and indeed eager for the dynamic of forgiveness to be set in motion again, but until I make the first move, we cannot begin to be reconciled. Such reconciliation is never cheap. It cannot happen until both parties recognize its cost and both recognize that each has found it costly—the one who has been offended by not falling back into the dynamics of coercive power above and the other by facing the hard task of truth-telling.

Such telling of the truth is certainly one of the keys—there is more than one on the ring of reconciliation. We hear this from those involved in conflict resolution and from the brave commission which has recently released its report in South Africa. It is so very difficult for all of us to "tell it like it is"—and tell it whole, neither justifying ourselves and leaving pointed (and therefore sharp) detail out nor abasing ourselves so much that we paint ourselves more damningly than we should.

My truth-telling, then, has to find a listening ear. You have to be willing to "pay" (the cost again) attention and receive my story, keeping your heart open as it learns to be forgiving over and over again (seventy times seven is the gospel total: that is a first century phrase meaning infinitely), not ignoring me, not rejecting me.

Ask yourself this: If that story about Jesus not condemning the woman caught in the act of adultery and bidding her to go and sin no more had been followed up with a similar incident involving the same woman, what would Jesus have said then? "You've had your chance; this time it's stoning" or "I cannot condemn you; you are again forgiven." What kind of look would she have seen in his eyes? Your answer will reveal much about what kind of God you really believe in.

The process of forgiveness and reconciliation demands courage from both of us. I am putting myself in your hands. You are now being challenged to exercise the love that is sure and steady, absorbing hurt and never being deflected by it and refusing to retaliate in a spirit of vengeance. It may also be that we both begin to recognize that the stories of our lives are not all that different and that they mingle: mine with yours and yours with mine.

That is anathema to those who want clear lines drawn and want the security of the opinion that they are completely in the right and most of humanity is completely in the wrong. But the process outlined is the only one that releases fresh energies of the compassion and lovingkindness that reaches deeper than strict justice, certainly deeper than rough justice.

Of course I can still block the process. I can refuse to receive your forgiveness. I can decide to wallow in my guilt, a neighbor to self-pity. When I do receive your forgiveness into my heart, I am deeply disturbed again, because you have seen the worst in me but have not condemned me, exiled me, or killed me. That implies that I have to die—die to my own worst self, the self that is self-justifying, manipulating, and controlling (or, as mirror opposite, self-condemning and self-hating). Condemnation, clear-cut lines, yes, that is much easier to live with. How dare you accept me as I am. You are saying that there is nothing I can do, nothing at all, to earn your love. I struggle with you; I try to refuse your offer; I do not want to look you in the eye which is enduring the hurts of my offense without looking (and throwing) daggers at me. How can I look into that eye without blanching and turning away, seared by your truth?

And again, how very hard for you to express that truth so that I see compassion along with the piercing, along with the scouring of the lie. Perhaps it is that the look is softened by your tears—

The "key" moment is simple, which is not to say it is easy. It is expressed in those three words which each of us has the power to use or not to use, *"I forgive you."* They echo those other deceptively simple words from the Gospels, "I visited you" (when you were in need). They take us far beyond the realm of coercive power, status, and skills. They are naked words of one human being to another. Forgive, visited—the words indicate the process: the life-giving, pain-bearing, lovemaking process of at-one-making. And it is I who remain steady where I am, not running away out of guilt or shame or fear, and it is you who no longer remain in your fastness, drawing back out of hurt, but who comes toward me.

Simple indeed. A moment of touch—a sacrament—ordinary in one way within the customs of public encounter, but conveying deeper meaning: it is the very instrument of release. We recognize that we are all broken. But it is in the embrace that we recognize the truth: we give each other freedom, the vulnerably open arms, trembling with new life, taking a risk that indeed we may be hurt again.

The touch goes along with the healing words, "I forgive you," and the silent wonder of the response, "You forgive me?" Doubtless it is followed by a drink or a meal—or even a love-making—that sets a seal on the reconciliation.

Such an exchange has the quality of eternal life. It is how we realize that we are in the divine domain here and now, because that is how it is to live in God's way, risen from our deadness, eased out of our stuckness, melted from our frozenness. Forgiveness brings release from blight and bane. The touch, the story, and the meal expand that forgiveness into reconciliation, because the playing field of power is level again.

It seems to me that we human beings usually (and indeed frequently) experience the processes of forgiveness and reconciliation in this way. It is not that God comes in as an extra element or that divine forgiveness is somehow altogether different. It is all of one piece, the human and the divine. Ours is the task of recognizing it and practicing it. It is incarnated: it is an enfleshed process. It is as we ourselves absorb the hurts of others that the divine forgiveness is worked out in the world of human relationships. The prayer that we may be forgiven our trespasses is not conditional on our being super-forgivers, but it works within the same dynamics of "as we forgive those who have trespassed against us." Of course none of us dare enter this mode, this dynamic, without being "breathed through" with the Holy Spirit, with the graciousness and courtesy of divine love.

But divine forgiveness does not come to us from "on high," from completely outside of us, or from a throne or a judgment seat. God never ceases to be actively engaged in forgiving: it is one way of describing the constancy and persistency of divine love. To be consistent with what has been shown to us of God through Jesus' example, we can never believe in ultimate exclusion and condemnation. God bears the pain of our refusal to see and admit our failures to love and bears the pain of our refusal to receive the releasing love that is always offered.

God endures as long as it takes: without that truth it is not possible for human beings to forgive God. For our accusation is placed alongside God's. Why, why, why do so many children have to die in agony? I need to hear a reply that says, "Forgive me for having created a world in which so much pain happens. I know of no other way to enable human beings in freedom to grow to love with a love worthy of the name." After Auschwitz and Hiroshima, forgiveness has become more difficult than ever. Dare we seem to be unorthodox enough to understand it as a two-way process between God and us? God, when will you justify your ways to us? It is certainly a cry of the heart, and I do not think it is blasphemy.

If we hear such a word from God, then we might be ready for the truth that God's very nature is to risk being unnoticed. Perhaps then we can recognize the divine presence that identifies with those who have been sinned against and demonstrates the intimacy, the healing touch, the releasing word, or the all-embracing meal that may be evidence enough that we are all held together in God and that nothing can separate us.

Those who "pronounce" do not move toward the ones who are affected by the pronouncement. They keep their distance; they do not soil their hands; they do not become involved; they keep others always at arm's length; they remain locked in their sense of superiority; they depend on their armies to control others; they stand on their dignity. They are unable to inhabit the divine milieu, where the air quality is such that we are always breathing forgiveness.

If we project such notions onto God, we create a monster in the image of our worst selves. If only the rule book and the practice of the churches could convince us that we have at last rid ourselves of such idolatry. So far only a few people have been able to say "yes" to the question Jesus reportedly asked his followers after he had laid aside his power and become like those who were unnoticed, stigmatized, and blamed. "Do you understand what I have done for you?" We may answer "yes" with our heads but rarely with our lives, and not yet in the corporate ways and structures of churches and societies.

Perhaps we can be too demanding of ourselves, but that truth about releasing and retaining forgiveness is demanding, and from the perspective of the divine presence as a vulnerable naked love, it is quite terrifying. Then again, the gifts of love always are.

Forgive but Don't Forget (Genesis 50:15-21)

Ronald E. Swisher

John F. Kennedy, according to Robert Dole in his book, *Great Political Wit*, said, "Forgive your enemies, but never forget their names."[1] It sounds like a reasonable statement. How about the comment Hillary Rodham Clinton supposedly made: "How many times did Jesus say to forgive? Seventy times seven? Well, I've been counting!"

Who could find fault with these remarks? It seems to me that to forgive does not mean that one is naïve or "Pollyanna" or oblivious to what is happening around one. I believe that both statements were made with some humor, although there is a cutting edge of truth in each.

We are to forgive, not just because God and Jesus and every major religious thinker and advocate from Buddha to Katori to Ram Das says so, but because, as health professionals tell us, it heals the person who forgives as much as it heals the person who is forgiven. I happen to be writing this at a time not long after the impeachment trial of President Clinton where he was acquitted. A reporter asked the President if he could forgive. He responded, "A person who asks for forgiveness must be willing to give it." Forgiveness is a dimension needed if one is to be a person who is whole, healthy, and full of well-being. Peace, serenity, and wholeness mark our lives when we can let go of resentment and anger.

In the Old Testament, Joseph is considered one of the great examples of putting forgiveness into practice. We know the story about how his brothers left him in a pit to die because they were jealous and envious of Joseph's gifted imagination and his power to interpret dreams (particularly the dream that had him ruling over his brothers and that they were subject to him). They left him but then went back and sold him into slavery. After that Joseph had days like many of us—up and down, down and up. He was placed in a pit—therefore, down. His brothers pulled him out of the pit—up. He was exalted by Pharaoh—up. But Pharaoh's wife, to put it in colloquial terms, wanted to "get down"—therefore, from being up, Joseph was placed down in the dungeon because he refused Pharaoh's wife. But, from down in the dungeon, he was brought up again because Pharaoh looked favorably on Joseph's ability to interpret the Pharaoh's dreams. That is what I mean about life being full of ups and downs—like a roller coaster. How do we handle our ups and downs? What should be our attitude?

I can imagine that Joseph was furious with his brothers. I do not think he stayed in the pit or the dungeon without thinking of how treacherously and wrongly he had been treated. It is human to feel devastated by someone's cruelty that has caused us misfortune. One must forgive, but the common admonition to forget seems unrealistic and beyond human to me. I believe that those who tell you that you should forgive after an unbelievable cruelty has been done to you would not be so quick to say that if they had the same experience. Forgiveness is not a natural response without some grace-filled intervention.

I do not subscribe to the premise that in order to forgive one must forget. To forget is not redemptive for the person being forgiven or the person offering forgiveness. This may go against what has been taught about forgiveness, but there is nothing wrong with praying for people and remembering their names. Furthermore, Joseph—during his ups and downs and downs and ups—expressed his hurt, his anger, and his frustration, too.

I am not advocating that a person should strike back or be bitter or let anger and resentment destroy one. But, I am saying that forgiveness is not easy, nor is it an automatic response. It takes practice. Perhaps that is why Jesus told us to forgive "seventy-seven times." Joseph was not so forgiving when he finally saw his brothers again. He wanted to punish them, and he played tricks on them at first. He seemed determined to pay them back for their betrayal and treachery. (Reread the story in Genesis.) What eventually happened, however, is that Joseph uttered those famous words: "Do not be afraid! Am I in the place of God? Even though you intended to do harm to me, God intended it for good, in order to preserve a numerous people, as he is doing today" (Genesis 50:19-20).

You meant it for evil, but God meant it for good. Could that be one of the keys to forgiveness? Do we keep count? Do we take names? Or does God intervene to make things eventually work for good?

One might wonder what I mean that one should forgive but not forget. Should the victims of the Holocaust forget the horrors of concentration camps and torture? Should Native Americans forget their genocide, or African Americans the enslavement of their race? Should victims of rape, incest, or abuse forget their hurt and pain?

What I am trying to say is that forgiveness is not the same as forgetting. Not to forget means, if possible, not permitting mistreatment to be repeated. It is not healthy or redemptive to allow injustice to continue, especially if it is because I have been oblivious, forgetful, or naïve, permitting openness and vulnerability, love, or forgiveness to encourage evil. I believe that forgiveness is possible without having one's memory impaired. Forgive, but don't forget!

Let me make these final observations: first, I recall the letter to the Ephesians, where the writer says, "Be angry but do not sin; do not let the sun go down on your anger, and do not make room for the devil" (4:26-27).

It is all right to get angry. Righteous anger—anger against injustice, oppression, and all the "isms" that deny people their freedom and humanity—is justified. But the kind of anger that one nurtures, cultivates, and "goes to bed" with is dangerous and takes away one's spirit, joy, and hope. When anger dominates to that degree, it allows the devil a foothold in one's heart.

It is the same with forgiveness. Not being able to forgive poisons one's spirit and heart. If Joseph had continued his masquerade, he would have been a casualty in this drama. We probably would not have heard of him again, at least not in the redemptive role he played. His example inspires us to look for the good in the midst of the worst circumstances and situations. Joseph's life encourages us to look to God to show us the good in our

135

dilemmas, heartaches, heartbreaks, mistakes, mess-ups, and mistreatments. Thank God for Joseph's insight, for his ability to forgive, and for his allowing God to take the worst and make something good come from it. How we respond to what happens to us is the key to fulfillment and victorious living.

Second, in worship we say, "God is good," and the response from the people is, "All the time!" If we can always respond in that way, then joy, hope, and love will be the attitude and experience of our lives. Our minds, our spirits, our inner lives depend so often on our attitude, on how we process what happens to us, good or evil.

We cannot exist in this world without forgiveness. Therefore, may we forgive and may the not forgetting be redemptive, too.

Note

1. Dole, R. (1998). *Great Political Wit*. New York: Doubleday.

Terrorism and Forgiveness

William J. Abraham

The eighth of November, 1987, was a regular Sunday in Dallas for my family until about half past four in the afternoon. We had been to church, eaten lunch, lounged around the house, watched a bit of football on television, chatted about the events of the week, and the like.

Then the dreadful news came through on CNN. There had been a bomb in my hometown of Enniskillen, Northern Ireland, that morning. It happened at the war memorial on Belmore Street. I knew almost every square foot of the area that had been devastated. In fact the first bicycle I ever owned had been bought in the cycle shop next door to the site of the savage killings. I had walked past the memorial hundreds of times, as I headed west—marking in my mind the bridge that led into the heart of the town, noting the convent school up on the hill, glancing across the glorious river Erne to catch a glimpse of the housing estate where we lived, and looking this way and that into the shops on each side of the street.

I flew into a stretch of intense concentration as I strained to hear and see every word and image that was projected across the world. This was not just another act of terrorism inflicted on innocent people. This was my town! Those killed and injured were not just names in the newspaper. These were people I knew from my childhood! Those destroyed and maimed were not distant and anonymous figures. These were people whose families I knew or whom I knew personally! I can still remember the smoke, the rubble, the frantic efforts of ordinary people and medical personnel to render service in the midst of chaos, the stories of terror, and the scenes of shock and horror.

I caught sight of uniformed members of Ballyreagh Silver Band, using their bare hands to clear away bricks and concrete to get to the dead and injured. I had been a member of the band as a schoolboy before I took off for university. Every year we had two parades on Armistice Day: one in Enniskillen and one in Fintona. The band had been part of the parade in Enniskillen that Sunday morning, as it headed up through Belmore Street. Then the bomb went off, perhaps prematurely. Once the suffering began there was nothing the band members could do but to tear open the rubble to get to the victims. To this day many of them tingle in their skin when they mull over what might have happened if they had taken the full blast of the bomb themselves.

I was dumbfounded as I watched it all, calling the family together to make sure they would not hear what had happened secondhand. We were speechless, holding our hands over our mouths in disbelief, our eyes darting from one to the other to share our sense of horror and outrage. I wanted immediately to reach for the phone and call my brother to get the details. In time I did, but for the moment we were riveted to the spot.

As the day progressed I could not get the sights, sounds, and suffering out of my mind. I was glued to CNN, preparing myself each time the news was repeated on the half hour to catch a scene or a comment that I had missed in the first encounter with the horror. Then, to my astonishment, I caught an interview with Gordon Wilson.

I had known "Mr. Wilson," as we called him, in my own church on Darling Street, the Methodist church where I was converted and called into the ministry in the classical Methodist manner. I knew his children from Sunday school, although we came from the "other side of the tracks," as the Americans would say. Gordon Wilson was not an especially pious person. He had a pronounced southern accent, and he was known in the town as an astute and eminently successful businessman.

That morning he had gone with his daughter, Marie, to watch the parade and remember the dead from the two world wars. With the other ordinary citizens who had gathered, they had taken the full force of the bomb. He had been injured but survived. His daughter had died holding his hand beneath the rubble. She was one of eleven who were killed that day.

Charlie Warmington, an old friend from school days, had arranged the interview with Gordon Wilson. It was crisp and clear. Buried under the concrete, somebody grabbed his hand. He described the situation with a minimum of elaboration.

It was Marie. Marie said, "Is that you, Daddy?"
I said, "Yes."
"Are you all right, Daddy?" she asked.
I said, "I'm fine."
Three or four times I asked her if she was all right, and each time she replied, "I'm fine, how are you?" I said, "Hold on. They will be coming to have us out soon."
Then she said, "Daddy, I love you very much." That was the last thing she said.

I have lost my daughter, and we shall miss her. But I bear no ill will, I bear no grudge. Dirty sort of talk is not going to bring her back to life. She was a great wee lassie. She was a pet, and she's dead. She is in Heaven, and we'll meet again. Don't ask me please for a purpose. I don't have an answer. But I know there has to be a plan. It's part of a greater plan, and God is good. And we shall meet again.

On my next visit home I went to see the Wilsons. On meeting Gordon after being gone for almost two decades, I found a man of extraordinary faith and integrity. He bore this tragedy, at least as far as outsiders could see, with great dignity and fortitude.

The events in Enniskillen are the tip of a massive iceberg of violence that has engulfed Northern Ireland for the last thirty years. As I write, the citizens of Omagh, another provincial town, are trying to put life back together after an even more atrocious bombing where twenty-nine people were killed and over three hundred injured. These are carefully orchestrated events that are planned and carried out with great deliberation. What is of interest here are the moral and theological dilemmas posed by these sorts of tragedies. The bombing of Enniskillen and Gordon Wilson's response to the death of his daughter provide a dramatic point of entry to a very tough set of issues that cry out for analysis.

We begin with the obvious. This was an act of vicious violence carried out against a group of innocent civilians. There is no way in which it can be morally justified; there are no extenuating circumstances to mitigate its brutality. All who seek to excuse the acts of violence involved or try to cover the truth of the situation in a fog of rhetoric are morally corrupt. The truth of the matter is clear: a heinous act of evil has been done.

Those who carried it out must be brought to justice. They deserve both the protection and the full weight of the criminal justice system. They deserve protection, because some of the victims or their families, will want to execute revenge by taking the law into their own hands. This is why Gordon Wilson's insistence that there be no "dirty talk" was precisely correct. They also deserve the full weight of the law in punishment, because such behavior is morally reprehensible, and it is rightly outlawed by the state.

Justice should be distinguished from therapy and from deterrence, both of which can be taken into account in its administration. Every effort should be made to heal the nefarious dispositions of these violent agents. However, they must be seen as agents rather than patients. They have chosen strategies for the execution of their intentions, and they have been trained, at great cost to themselves and others, to develop them. They are not victims; they are full-blooded agents.

Every effort should be made to administer justice in a manner that will deter them and others from engaging in murder and brutality. However, even while being punished for their crimes, they are persons with rights who are not to be used as the means to an end. They deserve the respect due to them as persons. Thus they are to be given such punishments as fit their crimes. When their punishment is complete, they are once more agents to be received back into society, with all the privileges of citizens restored to them. Moreover, through the administration of justice, there is always space both for mercy and for the consideration of mitigating circumstances. This is why justice can never be a matter of simple calculation; it must ultimately be in the hands of those who can take all the relevant factors into consideration.

To be sure this sort of analysis has often been challenged. On the one hand, pious sentimentalists are wont to see it as harsh. They mistake revenge for retribution, failing to note the crucial distinction that exists between a person paying back someone for harming them and a properly constituted system of law giving all persons the respect and rights they are due. On the other hand, some tough-minded postmodernists will be tempted to dismiss all law as the administration of raw power dealt out in the interests of those who control the system. They fail, in the process, to distinguish innocence from guilt. For them there can be no morally relevant distinction between the victim and the victimizer, everything is a matter of power and interests camouflaged as morality and order. In the end they would hand us all over to the crude forces of violence that stalk every civilization.

Is this the end of the matter? Is this not a recipe for the status quo? Does it not inhibit, or even render impossible, the kind of creative political process where there can be give-and-take on all sides so that peace may eventually be gained? Where do forgiveness, reconciliation, and peace fit into this picture? Can there be no way forward that will break the cycle of violence and open the door to a fresh start for everybody?

Take forgiveness first. Clearly this is a crucial first step in any possible reconciliation. What would it mean to forgive the Enniskillen bombers? Essentially it would involve three interrelated factors: deciding not to hold their brutality against them, abandoning any resentment for what they have done, and doing one's best to attend to their welfare. Obviously, this is a tall order, but this is surely the direction in which forgiveness lies.

The act of forgiveness spreads, in this case, across a range of people, beginning with those who are immediately involved, those who lost loved ones or were themselves injured. It can extend out to those more remotely involved, whose lives were affected in a host of negative ways. It can even reach as far as the families and communities of those who carried out the bombing, for some may be ashamed and distressed by what was done by those close to them. Forgiveness can be exercised by the community as a whole or that section of the community that the bombing was specifically directed toward.

141

Some people have suggested that forgiveness is not conceptually possible, that to forgive is to act in a confused and incoherent manner. To forgive is to adopt a set of positive attitudes toward the offender and to abandon certain negative ones. But some believe that to surrender such attitudes requires that one condone the original acts that set up the very conditions for forgiveness. Hence forgiveness is not possible; it fosters further moral wrong. So we should resist the temptation to forgive in the interests of intellectual coherence and moral duty.

I suspect that it is this kind of argument that lies at the base of the human tendency to shrink back from forgiveness, especially when the offense was morally outrageous. The grudging acknowledgment that in some cases one might forgive but most certainly not forget fits with this line of reasoning. Moreover, in those cases where it is psychologically difficult to separate the agent from the act, this proposal can easily become extremely attractive. In cases of horrendous evil, it is not easy to see how one can treat the offender as if nothing has happened. To forgive would appear to obliterate the distinction between the innocent and the guilty. It is small wonder that many find forgiveness a puzzling phenomenon.

One way to address this dilemma is to require that offenders change their ways before they are forgiven. Hence offenders must acknowledge their evil acts, express genuine sorrow and contrition, seek forgiveness of the offended party, repent, make reparation, and so on. Only where this happens can one begin to think of forgiveness. Where there is this kind of change, then it might be possible both to recognize fully the evil perpetrated and take up a positive attitude toward the offenders. After all the offenders have deliberately separated themselves from their evil acts, thus permitting the victim to see him or her in an entirely new light.

Even then, practicing forgiveness can be a tremendous challenge. At a personal level, it may be virtually impossible to eradicate the suffering inflicted by the offender from one's mind, so adopting a forgiving attitude is easier said than done. One may have genuine doubts concerning the sincerity and depth of change in the offender. When it comes to one community forgiving another, matters are even more complicated. In modern societies, there are virtually no recognized mechanisms for seeking corporate pardon for offenses committed. Communities are made up of a mixture of persons who may or may not join in the relevant acts of repentance and reparation; and communities can change quite drastically over the generations, so even identifying what a community does can be subject to debate and suspicion. It is no surprise, then, that dealing at a very basic level with forgiveness can easily appear to be an exercise in futile idealism. If forgiveness is the foundation of reconciliation and peace, then the situation is grim indeed.

Yet in the Christian tradition, we are commanded to forgive our enemies. Forgiveness is not a matter of choice; it is a matter of necessity. How can this be maintained given the obstacles that I have just identified?

It is tempting for well-meaning folk to press the necessity of forgiveness and reconciliation without coming to terms with the moral issues involved. I grew up in Northern Ireland at a time when the main Protestant churches were tempted to take this route. Church leaders often approached the problem laden with shame and guilt. After all, the troubles and their attendant violence were intimately tied to ethnic and nationalist disputes that were laced in turn with religious content and significance. It was hard not to sense that the church had been grievously at fault. As things got worse, it was natural to sharpen the call for forgiveness and reconciliation both as a solution to the current disruptions and as compensation for former complacency and complicity. This became all the more compelling when more belligerent voices set up their own church in order, it would seem, to poison the wells for their own political ends.

Over time I found that the constant round of calls for forgiveness and reconciliation rang hollow. The calls made next to no difference to the situation, and those who made them were easily exploited by those committed to violence and an idolatrous nationalism. As I follow the current efforts to trade prisoners for peace, it is difficult not to dismiss the whole process as a farrago of well-orchestrated confusion. I can only begin to imagine how difficult it is for a wife to see the murderer of her husband walk out of prison with financial stability and other benefits and take up residence again down the street. As I write

143

this, I continue to keep track of the punishment beatings that occur daily. Only yesterday it was reported that a gang of eight had entered a home in the early hours of the morning and cut the name of the man they wanted into the raw flesh of a young woman. Those who have promised again and again to take the gun out of politics in Northern Ireland in the name of forgiveness, reconciliation, and peace often refuse to face the consequences of their failed promises. There can be no forgiveness or reconciliation without justice. This is the nub of the matter.

The command to forgive, to seek peace, is a real one. How then is forgiveness and the pursuit of peace possible without falling victim to pious sentimentality and political illusion?

We begin by acknowledging the distinction between the offender and the offense. Human agents are made in the image of God, and they have been redeemed at great cost by the blood of Jesus Christ. Whatever they may have done, they have a dignity and a value that are distinct from their deeds. If the world cannot see this, the Christian believer does. Hence it is possible to hate the sin and love the sinner—this hackneyed adage is exactly right. Without this distinction we are doomed to hostility forever. Without condoning the evil perpetrated, we can be committed in positive ways to the agents of evil. We can forgive them, forgo the resentment we feel toward them, pray for them, and seek their best welfare. This is neither confused nor incoherent.

In the act of forgiving we are to see others from a divine point of view. Whatever they may have done, they are persons of incomparable worth merely because of creation and redemption. Their deeds are swallowed up in the divine reality. They are swamped in an ultimate reality that has been challenged by the brutality of human sin in the incarnation of the Son of God. Whether they acknowledge it or not, they are now bathed in the light of Easter and Pentecost and surrounded by moral and spiritual possibilities that are invisible to the secular eye. We ourselves have come to know this extraordinary forgiving reality in the grace of the gospel. We speak here not of some abstract set of principles but of a biting, vivid truth that has wormed its way into our hearts and minds.

We can go further. We all see things from our own point of

view with our passions and self-interest deeply engaged. Hence there is a need to temper our judgments and to leave all ultimate judgment in the hands of God. Just as no damage, even damage as extreme as death in this life, is the end of the matter because there is a life to come, so no judgment we make, however accurate, is the end of the matter. Judging is dangerous for by the judgment that we judge, so will we too be judged. This should temper all our moral deliberations. Indeed it is a matter of relief that we can leave all things in the hands of an ultimate Judge and Judgment that surpass our capacity in this life.

It is also good to recall that the age to come has already dawned; the future is already upon us, enacted in the liturgies of all our traditions. Pentecost is both a past event and a continuing reality; Christ has sent the promised Holy Spirit for the healing of nations. So we need not despair of the real victory, both within and without, over evil. Comprehensive moral, spiritual, and political renewal are always a possibility this side of Easter and Pentecost.

Hence we can tackle the command to forgive and love armed with resources from faith. Even while the evil is fully acknowledged, the agent of that evil is not reduced to the act, for we are more than what we do. All of us, both offender and offended, are enduring souls who count before God—whatever we have done or whatever has been done to us. The command to forgive is a veiled promise of grace that is sufficient for the day and the hour. So the paradox of forgiveness can be overcome. It is really possible both to acknowledge the evil done and be committed to the welfare of the evildoer.

Forgiveness may or may not lead to personal reconciliation. In situations where offenders refuse to mend their ways, clearly this will be impossible since reconciliation, unlike forgiveness, is essentially bilateral. There are also cases where it would be dangerous and foolish to enter into a relationship where one's own person or that of one's family will be at risk. One can certainly hope for reconciliation, and one can struggle to attain it, but not everything is possible here. The crux of the matter is that one is committed to the welfare of the offender come what may. When reconciliation occurs, it is a matter for rejoicing; when it does not, then regret, or even lament, is in order.

The transition from this mode of being and acting to the next requires circumspection. It is often thought that to forgive also requires that the offended party relinquish all thought of reparation or punishment. This is mistaken. Our obligations at this level are complex. If a person deliberately harms another, it is only right that he or she be obligated to make reparations when possible. The person harmed may forgo reparation, but there is no obligation to do so. In some circumstances such behavior may be heroic, exhibiting a conspicuous goodness that overflows our ordinary moral requirements. In some circumstances, it may be the demand of the offender that he or she be allowed to make reparation, and this should surely be permitted. This may in itself be essential for the healing and welfare of the offender.

In cases where criminal activity is involved, then the situation is entirely different. Just as persons have no right to take the law into their own hands in order to right a wrong done against them, persons have no right to waive the requirements of the law when a wrong has been done against them. Those in power are apt to ignore this when they are surrounded by evil. They can readily reach for the language of forgiveness and reconciliation as a way to escape the legal consequences of their actions. When this action is skillfully presented in quasi-religious settings, it is easy for ordinary people to become confused (a fact not ignored by spin masters and politicians). However, the whole point of the law is to take the issue of justice out of the hands of the offended so that there may be an impartial rendering of what is due. To be sure, the legal system can take into account how things stand between the offender and those offended, but this is far from abandoning the requirements of justice. Forgiveness and justice are radically different concepts; they stand whole and complete on their own. To draw on forgiveness to undermine justice is to pave the way for further evil. It also runs the risk of undermining that fragile but real moral order that should be embodied within the legal system.

We can see, then, how challenging it is to insist on forgiveness without falling into legal or political illusion. There is a place for the dramatic display of reconciliation between estranged parties. We are sorely in need of ways and means to bring contending parties together and induce them to work things through after the generations of brutality and terrorism. It is good to devise tribunals and procedures where victims can confront those who have harmed them or where offenders can publicly acknowledge their evil and express their repentance. Yet it is too easy to be morally blinded by the splendid drama and by the acts of conspicuous goodness that can emerge in such instances. The very existence of such mechanisms requires the sanction and protection of the law. They presuppose a commitment to justice and morality; they cannot replace either. Nor can they eradicate the stubborn stratagems of sin and evil that are so pervasive in our world.

Even with these qualifications in place, the search for peace and reconciliation between estranged parties will be demanding. Beyond the quest for forgiveness, reconciliation, and justice, there is a host of matters to be worked through. It is not difficult to draw up a laundry list of desiderata for Northern Ireland, so we need goodwill on all sides. We need stable structures that can provide time and space for trust to grow and flourish. We need protection from paramilitary gangs and psychopaths. We need a full generation of cultural interaction between northern and southern Ireland. We need accurate renderings of our histories, cleansed of ancient myths and legends. We need a massive encounter with that ancient Christian past that existed long before there were Protestants or Roman Catholics in the land. We need to eradicate the infrastructure of terrorism that still exists and the cult of violence that fosters it. Forgiveness cannot stand proxy for such matters; but it can certainly create space for their existence. Even terrorists can and should be forgiven. Happily this can be done without undermining that moral sensibility without which no forgiveness is possible and without abandoning that justice that no society can flourish without for long.

Forgiveness: Removing the Roadblocks

Michael H. Collins

F orgiveness is an issue in all our lives. Fights between siblings and spouses, feuds between neighbors, and the wrongs endured by victims of crime are but some of the events that might challenge us to forgive. But we may have given little serious thought to what forgiveness means since we sat in Sunday school hearing about the prodigal son, wishing our dad had been as understanding about that time when we took off with our friends and left Mom at home with the chores not done.

Many of us have a set of ideas about the Christian teaching on forgiveness left over from childhood, but when we try to apply them as adults we find they do not match up to reality and, far from fixing it, may make a problem worse. We believe we have to forgive quickly and completely, forgetting entirely about the injury we have suffered (always supposing, of course, that those who wronged us want to be forgiven). If we cannot forgive in this way, we fear God will not forgive us. We start off feeling bad as the injured party, but it soon looks as if we are the ones who are going to be in trouble—with God.

As if that is not a tough enough bind, our stock of half-remembered childhood notions does not tell us anything about how forgiveness is going to help us avoid getting hurt again. We may assume that forgiveness also means reconciliation. But do we have to go on meekly accepting our boss's harassment or living with an abusive spouse? Do we have to do business again with someone who lied to us or cheated us? Does forgiveness somehow mean that what the person did was not wrong, and we were maybe worse than they were because we became angry or resentful? What are we supposed to do with our outraged feelings? And so we go on, puzzled and miserable, not getting anywhere with the issue in hand. Assumptions like these make it hard for us genuinely to forgive. They put roadblocks in our way.

Books like this one are written to meet the need to sort out what forgiveness involves and what religion teaches. According to the Barnes & Noble catalogue, there are more than two hundred books about forgiveness on the market in the United States. Among the authors who have recently written helpful books are: Lewis B. Smedes, Robert Brizee, Beverly Flanigan, Robin Casarjian, Robert M. Libby, Sidney B. Simon, and Suzanne Simon. Most of the books in the catalogue are written by Christians, but one I have found especially helpful is *How Good Do We Have to Be?* by Rabbi Harold S. Kushner. He discusses Bible stories about wrongdoing and forgiveness (such as the garden of Eden, Cain and Abel, and the prodigal son) from the point of view of an adult religious believer who has needed to forgive and to counsel others on how to do so.

Let me be clear about the sort of resources Christianity offers to people wrestling with the issue of whether, and on what terms, to forgive. Christianity is not a theory. It is not, for example, simply an explanation of the problem of evil and why the need for forgiveness arises—although it has much to say about God, humankind, and the world, and about justice, grace, and love.

Christianity is first and foremost, as the earliest believers proclaimed, a way of life based on a relationship to God known through Jesus Christ and lived in community. Christianity is a response to the God who, in Jesus, even suffered death for us, forgiving those who brought that death about and creating a new Kingdom that we can join through the resurrection of Christ from the dead. To people whom injustice and conflict so often leave broken and bleeding, sometimes literally (like Jesus on the cross), the Christian life offers a way for healing, forgiveness, and renewal to build our lives anew. These resources are sometimes referred to as "bread" by the Christian tradition. For broken lives, there is broken bread given out and shared;

bread that increases and multiplies the more it is shared, the bread of eternal life which continually gives our true life back to us. Now let's examine five roadblocks we may encounter on the way to forgiveness.

Roadblock No. 1: A Christian has to forgive quickly and completely.

Forgiving quickly and completely is not realistic or required. This roadblock occurs when we think too much in terms of law and penalties. Forgiveness is a process of inner healing. When we have a physical sickness, we may need to take medication, change our diet, receive counseling, or practice exercises. Sometimes we have to change the type or mix of healing agents. We certainly need to give time for the healing to take place. Some years ago I was prostrate with a minor back injury and in intense pain. The doctor tried one medication after another without effect. Finally he tried a third that worked wonderfully. "Your body knows what it needs," he said. "Sometimes it takes trial and error to find the right remedy." So it is with healing ourselves. We need to take time to do three things. The first is to face the injury we are suffering and admit what it is and in what way it is hurting us. Second, we need to analyze what we need to have happen to overcome the hurt. Third, perhaps with the help of other people, we need to plan ways to rebuild our damaged self-esteem. When we have sufficient self-esteem we are more likely to be able to let go of our ill will and make the positive decision to forgive.

At that point, the sickness, perhaps akin to a fever that has had hold of us, relaxes. We are then ready to move to the next stage in the road to convalescence, rehabilitation, repaired communion with ourselves, God, and the world. It is especially helpful then to practice paying attention to the good that is all around us. Some go to view mountains, sail on the sea, or walk in gardens or the forest. Others look at pictures or listen to music.

The common factor is letting ourselves be taken up by beauty, power, and goodness. Such experiences naturally merge into prayer and enrich our prayer at other times. We come to see in

151

a different light, finding ourselves giving thanks for what we receive and loving ourselves and others more. It is most productive when those experiences challenge us, even make us a little uncomfortable. It is then, especially, that we are growing inner resources. We experience the gift of grace, which is part of what the New Testament means by "the bread of life." In time we find, almost without realizing, that we feel differently about our injury. Our lives are no longer defined by the wound we received or the injustice we experienced. The severe pain has receded from immediate memory. We have received the gift of being able to forgive.

Roadblock No. 2: It is impossible to forgive someone who does not repent.

When we are angry and hurt, we may feel that justice demands the other person repent before we forgive, but this confuses the other person's need to take responsibility for his or her actions with our responsibility to bring the right attitude to a relationship. While we wait for the other person to repent, we remain unhealed and likely still in pain. In that way we give the person who wronged us more power over our lives. By holding on to hurt, we make the original action worse, which does not serve the cause of justice.

Roadblock No. 3: A Christian should always try to forgive and forget.

The advice of the old proverb is appealing. But, humanly speaking, it is almost impossible to forget a serious injury—and with good reason. Telling ourselves to forgive and forget is likely to get us lost on two detours. The first takes us away from what forgiveness really is, a process of healing (Roadblock No. 1).

Pretending that an injury somehow did not happen or did not really matter when it did is simply burying it, and we cannot truly resolve the problem or forgive the person who hurt us. We may say words of forgiveness, but if we have not faced and dealt with the injury and allowed ourselves to receive the capacity to forgive, we are deceiving ourselves and others, adding untruth to the hurt. An unhealed injury is like a wound that has been prematurely closed. It is likely to fester and break open again worse than before.

If we fall sick, the doctor needs to take a history, note the symptoms, make a diagnosis, and prescribe a remedy. Similarly, when we are wounded within ourselves we need to remember the injury, what it was, and who was responsible and honestly assess how it is hurting us. Only by facing the truth of what happened can we realistically start on the road to real healing and true forgiveness.

We also need to learn from our injuries to try to protect ourselves and others from being hurt in that way again. Was there anything in our own behavior that, although not responsible for what happened, might have led to it? Sometimes the way we act permits others to believe that they can behave in ways that wrong us because forgiving is confused with condoning. Many years ago a guy bad-mouthed me for reasons I could not understand. I sought advice and allowed myself to be persuaded to forgive and forget. The result was that I ended up humiliated, and he went right on doing it. Fortunately our ways parted before significant harm was done. But by trying to forget and not taking steps to confront the matter, I ended up with an unresolved problem and two people to forgive.

We might understand the proverb more helpfully if we took the "forgive" to mean "accept the need for healing and undergo it" and "forget" to refer to the release that then comes from the feelings of pain we associate with our injury. It only makes sense to forget if reconciliation has taken place as well as forgiveness, and that is not always possible or desirable.

Roadblock No. 4: Genuine forgiveness means reconciliation and reunion with the person who wronged us.

A further roadblock to reaching forgiveness and peace is posed by the idea that forgiveness means behaving as if the injury had never happened. A Christian, we may tell ourselves, has to try to make everything the way it was before. Forgiving takes one person, the forgiver, to open the way in himself or herself to the possibility of reconciliation. But reconciliation takes two people, the forgiver and the forgiven. For forgiveness to turn into reconciliation, the injurer must accept responsibility for the injury and desire reconciliation. But does that contradict what was said about Roadblock No. 2? No, forgiveness is a way to our own inner peace, a means to stop the original wrong from doing more harm in our lives and to people we relate to. Forgiveness does not require or authorize us, in effect, to run other peoples' lives. They are free, like us, to go on their own journey.

If reconciliation takes place without a real resolution of the original issue, the relationship will most likely break down again or at least be unhappy and mutually destructive. It is failure to resolve the original issues in marriage, for example, that causes such a high proportion of subsequent marriages to fail. One couple I know separated because the wife, whose earnings bankrolled her husband's attempts to start up a business, grew tired of his failures and his lack of appreciation of what she was doing for him. Their lack of income prevented them from having the family she wanted. He said he was learning from his failures and would eventually succeed. After a series of rows, they agreed to separate. But when the husband's business at last began to take off, he tried to persuade his wife to return. Meanwhile she had made a new life that offered her financial security and the prospect of a family. She did not return, but they did forgive each other for the disappointment each had inflicted and they remain good friends. Both practiced forgiveness. Reconciliation was a step too far. They could not turn back the clock, but forgiveness made the future happier for both of them.

Roadblock No. 5: If some of the old angry feelings return, the original forgiveness was not valid.

Believing that the original forgiveness was not valid because old angry feelings return is too big a burden to lay on oneself. Often there are different levels of hurt and anger within a person. We may believe we have forgiven because we have found peace, but then something triggers fresh pain or resentment.

That does not mean the forgiveness was not genuine but that, for some reason, our original understanding and analysis did not go deep enough. That is no cause for despair. It simply means we have more work to do. And the God who helped us do that work before will enable us to do this also and be there to help us persevere until we see it accomplished.

A clearer road to forgiveness

When we began considering the road to forgiveness, we recalled childhood ideas and realized they were inadequate. Confronting the roadblocks created by these ideas, we have come to see the issue of forgiveness in broader terms than law and justice. A legalistic approach proves a short road to a dead end. The law declares what is right and by enforcing it, restrains and punishes wrongdoers. Although the law may compensate the injured to some extent, it cannot heal hurts, restore relationships, or deal with our feelings. In any case, there are times when we all fall short of what the law requires. Things look different when we are the ones in need of forgiveness. Taking a realistic approach to what has happened and undergoing inner healing may mean a long and painful journey, but it is the road to peace, joy, and hope.

The last and greatest roadblock we may need to clear is an unwillingness to be healed. If we have been unjustly injured, the way we were hurt may show us something about ourselves we would rather bury than face. Christianity tells us that God is a healer who comes to us graciously whenever and however often we ask. Working through the Holy Spirit, it is God who shows us the roadblocks on our personal route, who gives us the courage to face them and the strength to clear them away. We may suffer as God's grace fights a healing battle within us—and part of us may die a little, like tissue dies around a wound—but we have the promise of Christ that the One who raised him from the dead will also raise us, forgiving and forgiven, to newness of life.

The Forgiven Also Forgive

Paschal M. Baumstein

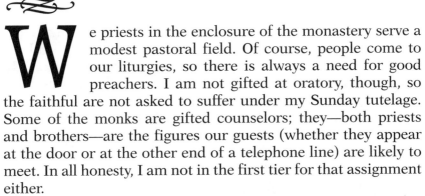

We priests in the enclosure of the monastery serve a modest pastoral field. Of course, people come to our liturgies, so there is always a need for good preachers. I am not gifted at oratory, though, so the faithful are not asked to suffer under my Sunday tutelage. Some of the monks are gifted counselors; they—both priests and brothers—are the figures our guests (whether they appear at the door or at the other end of a telephone line) are likely to meet. In all honesty, I am not in the first tier for that assignment either.

For whatever reason, some abbot in years past decided that the best place for me was in the confessional. My theory has long been that this assignment has nothing to do with any supposed gift of discernment, insight, or compassion on my part. In all probability, a wise superior reflected on the anonymity of the confessional and concluded that I, of all people, belonged in just such a setting.

Of course, I have no way of knowing how helpful I may have been in this work. I can, however, see its effect on me. The hours in the confessional have never failed to buoy me. To some people, the confessional probably seems a forum for countless sins, but for me it has always stood for a house of forgiveness, the place—the "ordinary means" as theologians would say—for absolution. I see person after person enter its precincts burdened but leave with a lightness that is surely indebted to his or her changed circumstances.

The common practice of confessors is to beg, upon parting, the penitent's prayers. I certainly hope that they pray for me, but

I have never been able to convince myself that their last moments in the confessional should center on *my* needs. So I reverse the ordinary procedure, promising instead that I will pray for them.

My perspective springs from something I learned from my father. Now, my mother was a woman of the deepest sympathy. She lived to serve, to help, and to aid. When we were sick as children, she was a full-time nurse, supplying us with distractions, comforts, and a ready ear. My father, while no less compassionate, had a different response, and I think that I am cast in his mold. Whereas Mother was sympathetic, Father was empathetic. Frankly, he was not very good at ministering to our pain; instead, he experienced our suffering, seemingly as fully as we did. In the process, or so it always appeared to me, he seemed to bear, in some measure, the weight of our affliction. I always think in particular of a time when I was ten. A brick wall fell on me. Mother busied herself removing bricks and trying to comfort me as we awaited the ambulance; Father, however, was virtually disabled by the pain. I think it was, in its own way, a profound—albeit rather corporeal—example of the Communion of the Saints: such was the spiritual bond between us that he took his son's pain as his own.

As a priest, I find a similar bond created in the confessional. Of course that sacred absolution, given through no merit of my own, surpasses anything I personally could contribute. Yet there is still some ongoing service that I can try to give—perhaps even more as a monk than as a priest—by bearing (at least in prayer) some small measure of their pain, their struggle to do better. Even after absolution, one needs to be commended to the Lord's providential oversight, to God's continuing care and attention. I take that as an aspect of my own small role in the penitent's forgiveness.

You can tell, I suspect, that I am consistently edified in the confessional—seeing there the thirst for rectification, the careful preparation of most of those who come to the monastery for the sacrament. Nonetheless, it always surprises me when one particular element is omitted. People come in; they admit their guilt; they profess their resolution to do better in the future; they request absolution. But that sequence contains a serious flaw, a missing element. What is so often overlooked is that the virtue here lies not in guilt but in contrition. A confessor is unlikely to ask, "Did you really do that?" He will see instead that the pivotal query is, "Are you *sorry* for your sins?" Contrition, after all, is the issue whereby one seeks forgiveness.

Presumably, by the penitent's entry into the confessional, guilt has already been conceded. Yet, for some reason, people seem inclined to dwell more prominently upon the issue of guilt than upon contrition. And that can be a serious problem, because instead of emphasizing the resolution to amend one's life, it rivets the person's focus upon his distraction from God.

For confession to meet its function fully, acting as a true rite of forgiveness, both the confessor and the penitent must manifest a crucial virtue: innocence. Sadly, that virtue is not often stressed today; nevertheless, it is, I earnestly believe, a key to real forgiveness. Grasping this concept, however, requires that one forsake those misleading concepts that commonly cling to innocence and consider instead its real meaning. As a virtue, innocence is *not* gullibility, nor does it refer to one's supposed lack of personal fault or sin. Innocence is far simpler, and—as is true of all virtues—its design rests within divinity. By the virtue of innocence, we mean no more than (1) believing in God—really believing in God—and (2) acting accordingly. Innocence entails acceptance of the fact that our Lord is all good, that all that God does is good and for the good, that the Lord never veers from the righteous path, and that God exercises providential care over creation. Despite what our cynical and skeptical world may suggest, this does not shroud reality. To the contrary, it accepts Saint Anselm's principle that, since God is absolute Truth, God is absolute Reality; thus genuine reality resides in whatever is closest to and most consistent with God. God, after all, is the Creator of all that is real. Thus whatever is at odds with God—with God's goodness, truth, and beauty—is at odds with reality. As Anselm articulated it, nothing is true except by participating in the divine Truth, and one is truer the closer one is to God. From this perspective, sin and offense of any kind are not "the way of the real world." Rather, they are deviations, aberrations; and as such, they merit neither indulgence nor acquiescence. The revelatory influence of innocence—because it refocuses a person on God and away from whatever offends God—readies the penitent (the forgiven) to be one who also forgives: an important dimension of the process.

At the beginning of the twentieth century, Monsignor Robert Hugh Benson (a man who today is best known for being the only son of an Anglican Archbishop of Canterbury who ever entered the Church of Rome) was a confessor of note and high repute. He wrote over forty works, many being pious fiction. In the stage version of one of his novels, *Come Rack! Come Rope!*, there is a confession scene that expresses this understanding of contrition as the handmaiden of forgiveness. In the course of the confession, the priest says to his penitent:

> The point, Robin, is that I do not judge you at all. Scripture forbids us to judge, lest we be judged in return. I stand here, because God has entrusted to Peter, and through Peter to me, the keys. With these keys I can unlock the door of mercy. But the keys provide no magic portal of perception and cognizance. They give me no faculties to judge guilt, just contrition. These keys are for forgiveness, and I cannot judge for what you can be forgiven. If you are sorry for your sins, I unlock the door, and you are forgiven. But if you do not even know your sins, you cannot be sorry for them, and I—who have no ability to judge in your stead—have naught to unlatch on your behalf.[1]

This passage contains a host of principles that figure into forgiveness, each tied to innocence: refusal to pass judgment, recognition of the limits of perception, a ready acceptance of the sorrow, and the contrition that one expresses. All of these factors are practiced naturally and ordinarily when one exercises the virtue of innocence.

And that is why innocence is such a mighty virtue. If embraced wholeheartedly and beneficently, it opens one's eyes to God, eliminating the brutal cynicism that tries to masquerade as realism or practicality. Indeed, a large measure of innocence's service is its purification of perspective. By unencumbering one's perception of both reality and divinity's role in reality, innocence enables the soul to forgive more readily, to forgive as an ordinary course. It allows forgiveness to be manifested, as

Saint Benedict remarks of humility, "natural[ly] and as if by habit, practice[d] always . . . out of love of the Lord, goodness of habit, and delight in virtue."[2] That is important. For were forgiveness no more than an occasional indulgence of some supposed magnanimity, it would have no foundation. Remember that genuinely Christian forgiveness is never an exception to ordinary practice because, rather than a mere act of will, it is an act of love.

The Roman Sacramentary includes a particularly insightful prayer, in its votive Mass "For Our Oppressors." It reads,

Father,
according to your law of love
we wish to love sincerely all who oppress us.
Help us to follow the commandments of your new covenant,
that by returning good for the evil done to us,
we may learn to bear the ill-will of others out of love for you.[3]

In the confessional, I have often referred people to this prayer. In my—admittedly limited—experience, I have found that when people pray "for" their enemies, all too often they are inclined to pray that their foes will change their way of thinking, that they will be converted, even that they will be "justly" punished or removed. But, the church proposes a very different prayer for our "oppressors." Instead—with absolute fidelity to the gospel— the entreaty here is that God will help us to love our oppressors, that those afflicting us will find us returning good for their evil, and that the oppression heaped upon us may be borne out of love of the Lord. This is a prayer of innocence; it is a prayer of forgiveness.

We all ought to respond to the lessons of this prayer. Forgiveness is not just a matter of saying "That's all right" or even a perfunctory "I forgive you." In the Christian dispensation, forgiveness is only genuine when it is suffused with love. Forgiveness is not passive, not some idle quality that we allow to surface as required. It is an active response. It is love of enemies, not mere toleration. According to the example of Christ, it is not satisfied by simply muttering "I accept your apology." Instead, one must boldly and truly profess "I love you; I bear no animosity regarding what passed between us; I do not just tolerate your acts, I embrace you in the love of Christ." The difference between these options is great and significant, because this difference is hinged upon whether one focuses upon oneself or upon the Lord.

Forgiveness always focuses upon the Lord.

Notes

1. Found in unsigned and undated manuscript in the archives of Belmont Abbey (North Carolina, United States). The quotation is from Act I, Scene 2, on p. 21. The stage version is based on Benson's novel of 1912.

2. Fry, T., ed. (1981). *RB 1980: The Rule of St. Benedict in Latin and English with Notes.* Collegeville, MN: The Liturgical Press, pp. 200-03 (7:68-69).

3. International Commission of English in the Liturgy, trans. (1974). *Missali Parvum e Missali Romano* (1970). Collegeville, MN: The Liturgical Press, p. 836.

Recommended Readings on Forgiveness

Augsburger, D. W. (1996). *Helping People Forgive*. Louisville: Westminster John Knox.

Enright, R. D. & North, J. (1998). *Exploring Forgiveness*. Madison: University of Wisconsin Press.

Flanigan, B. (1992). *Forgiving the Unforgivable*. New York: Macmillan.

Girard, R. (1985). *The Scapegoat*. Baltimore: Johns Hopkins University Press.

Keen, S. (1986). *Faces of the Enemy*. San Francisco: Harper & Row.

McCullough, M. G., Sandage, S. J., & Worthington, E. L. (1997). *To Forgive Is Human: How to Put Your Past in the Past*. Downers Grove, IL: InterVarsity.

Meninger, W. A. (1998). *The Process of Forgiveness*. New York: Continuum.

Patton, J. (1985). *Is Human Forgiveness Possible?* Nashville: Abingdon Press.

Study Guide

Lesson One: Stumbling Blocks to Forgiveness

Scripture: For if you forgive others their trespasses, your heavenly Father will also forgive you; but if you do not forgive others, neither will your Father forgive your trespasses. (Matthew 6:14-15)

Session Objective: To better understand what motivates and hinders us in forgiving.

Materials Needed: Pen and paper for written reflections during Personal Reflection Time.

Discussion Questions

1. Why is it important to forgive others? What benefits are gained from offering forgiveness? What happens to you when you refuse to forgive? What happens to the person you forgive?

2. What has being forgiven done for you? Think back upon a time in your life when you needed to be forgiven. What happened? Was it harder to *ask* for forgiveness or to fully *receive* another's forgiveness?

3. Christians often believe forgiveness to be a clear-cut, one time event. You ask, and you are forgiven. Someone asks for your forgiveness, and you say the words, "You are forgiven." But what if feelings of guilt or resentment resurface? Has forgiveness failed to work or is forgiveness a process?

4. Barbara Brown Taylor tells us there are two motivations for forgiving:

   ✓ We forgive because we have been forgiven ourselves, and God expects us to do unto others as God has done to us.

✓ We owe it to ourselves since bitterness and resentment will emotionally and spiritually deform us.

Which of these motivations has compelled you to forgive someone? Are there other motivations to let someone off the hook after they have hurt us?

5. If forgiveness is an act of transformation, what parts of yourself are you most afraid will change if you let go of the harm someone has done to you? If you give up your "unassailable rightness," what will you be left with? Why is it difficult to let go of the pain someone else has inflicted upon us? Why is it so hard to forgive ourselves for the painful consequences we have caused by our own bad choices?

6. Are some sins unforgivable? What would you find impossible to forgive, and why do you consider some sins more heinous than others? Basil Pennington says some sins are unforgivable in our human strength and understanding. He suggests that we pray, "Lord, I forgive everyone as fully as I can," knowing that God can continue the work when we cannot. When you imagine someone who has done the unforgivable, do you find these words helpful?

7. Why is praying for those who hurt us important? Pennington says that praying for those who hurt us helps us gain some distance from our pain and increases our ability to see those who hurt us as sinners who have been sinned against by others. Why would having compassion on our enemies help us forgive them?

8. Do you think there is a way to prepare our hearts for living a life of forgiveness? Halbert Weidner suggests that we prepare to forgive in advance when we learn not to judge others or cling to possessions. He writes, "Not judging and not accumulating property that can be harmed leaves us rather free from most of the probable causes of needing to forgive others." Do you think these two practices could help reduce or ease the need for offering forgiveness? Why or why not?

Personal Reflection Time

Review Michael Collins's "Roadblocks to Forgiveness."
- A Christian has to forgive quickly and completely.
- It is impossible to forgive someone who does not repent.
- A Christian should always try to forgive and forget.
- Genuine forgiveness means reconciliation and reunion with the person who has wronged us.
- If some of the old, angry feelings return, the original forgiveness was not valid.
- We would rather bury a terrible hurt than allow it to be healed through forgiveness.

Select one of the six roadblocks. On a piece of paper spend five minutes reflecting on how this roadblock has hindered you and what you believe to be true about how forgiveness really takes place. Here is an example:

Roadblock #1 says, "A Christian has to forgive quickly and completely." I remember when I tried to forgive A for spreading those rumors about me. I prayed to forgive her, but for months, every time I saw her, my rage returned. I wanted to hurt her back. I thought something was wrong with my faith. But looking back, I realized that I kept praying for the strength to forgive her again and again. Eventually I went and talked to her, and now I don't harbor any hard feelings toward her. I now believe that it doesn't matter how much time forgiveness takes. My faith isn't based on time limits. With God's help I can forgive those who have hurt me.

Closing Prayer

Pray the Lord's Prayer, taking time to pause and read the added text where indicated. If you are in a group setting, a leader can read aloud the sections in parentheses.

Our Father in heaven,
hallowed be your name,
your kingdom come,
your will be done,
on earth as in heaven.

Give us today our daily bread.
Forgive us our sins
(Have you knowingly hurt anyone's feelings this week? Have you dismissed anyone's ideas as worthless or ignored honest requests for help? If you have not given someone the dignity they are due as a child of God this week, please take this time to confess it and ask for forgiveness.)
   as we forgive those who sin against us.
(Pause and ask: Who has hurt you? Who do you feel owes you something? Who has violated your life in some way, making you feel used or unimportant? Please take this time to place that person and that situation in God's hands as you ask for the strength to forgive.)
Save us from the time of trial,
   and deliver us from evil.
For the kingdom, the power, and the glory are yours
   now and for ever. Amen.

Lesson Two: Attitudes of Forgiveness

Scripture: Do not judge, and you will not be judged; do not condemn, and you will not be condemned. Forgive, and you will be forgiven. (Luke 6:37)

Session Objective: To explore the attitudes and emotions that often are associated with forgiveness.

Materials Needed: Pen and paper for written reflections during Personal Reflection Time.

Discussion Questions

1. Can forgiveness be harmful to us? Roberta Bondi thinks it can if we believe forgiveness means we must say to our injurers, "It is all right that you have attacked my self; I shouldn't have one anyway." How might believing yourself unworthy of dignity or fair treatment affect your understanding of forgiveness? How might a healthy self-identity as a loved child of God enhance your ability to forgive?

2. Roberta Bondi writes that forgiveness has two difficult requirements:

    ✓ Give up the idea of revenge against our injurers or of holding them accountable to pay back every bit of the "debt" they owe us.

    ✓ Pray for the well-being of those who spitefully use us.

    Which of these "requirements" is more difficult to you? Can you think of other "requirements" of forgiveness?

3. Read Matthew 18:21-22. Why do you think Jesus tells Peter to forgive another person in the church seventy-seven times? Are hurts inflicted by other Christians harder to forgive? What about hurts inflicted by others close to us, such as family members?

4. Monica Furlong describes the "odd tightening of the lips, the glare, the huffiness, the occasional banging of saucepans" that were common expressions of anger in her household as she grew up. Putting anger into words was not permitted. How was anger dealt with in your family of origin? How do you deal with anger now?

5. Furlong goes on to write that anger is "one of the great human sources of energy and action" and "a very important indicator...[that] warns us that a relationship between us and another person or group of persons is beginning to go wrong." Can you think of a time when your anger served to warn you? Can you think of another time when you nursed your anger and it turned to bitterness?

6. In the face of terrible wrongs, does forgiveness demean or ignore those who have been maimed, killed, or forever marked by evil deeds? Should some evils not be forgiven so they won't be forgotten or repeated?

7. Margaret Hebblethwaite writes, "The ultimate message of forgiveness is this: What you have done is so terrible that nothing like that must ever be allowed to happen again on this earth. Every fiber of my being and every ounce of my

energy must be turned to fighting this evil. To put a stop to such things happening I will break the cycle. Instead of repaying injury with injury, hurt with hurt, I will put a spoke in the wheel of revenge and stop it dead in its path. The cycle is broken." Do you see a connection between the things you have had to forgive and the social justice issues that most concern you? Can you see your ability to forgive as a tool for bringing good into the world?

8. What do you do if you just can't get along with someone? Is reconciliation necessary for those you simply don't relate with or who have hurt you repeatedly? Can you just wish others well in their lives and go on with yours without them in it? Is this a loving option?

9. William Willimon writes, "Jesus is not only the one who urges forgiveness; Jesus is also the one who embodies forgiveness." How did Jesus embody forgiveness? How did he treat those who persecuted him? What did he say to those who crucified him? How do Jesus' life and words challenge our understanding of forgiveness?

Personal Reflection Time

Exercise One: Reread the monk's story retold by Roberta Bondi on page 34, then spend a few moments answering the following questions in writing.

- Has a "wilderness of thistles and thorns" grown in your life?
- Are there hurts from your past that you don't want to deal with? What are they?

Be as specific as possible. Try to list two things you can do today to begin to forgive or let go of hurts that you have neglected to deal with.

These are the hurts that I need to forgive:
Example: I need to forgive my sister for bringing her new boyfriend to my son's confirmation party when I told her it was just for immediate family members.

This is what I can do today to begin to forgive:
Example: (1) I can write in my journal to let out my anger at my sister. She took the attention away from my son on his special day by not paying attention to my wishes. She embarrassed her boyfriend and me by putting us in a situation when both of us knew I hadn't reserved a place for him and when those closest to my son shared intimate memories of him that her boyfriend did not share. (2) I can call my sister next week after I've simmered down and tell her I am working through my feelings and want to forgive her and put this behind us.

Exercise Two: What daily discipline of prayer might you add to your life to help you begin the slow process of forgiveness? Bondi suggests praying with the psalms and gospel stories or silent prayer that involves simply sitting in silence as prime avenues of prayer that bring awareness and healing. Here are other suggestions: Each morning as you get dressed you might simply pray, "Lord, have mercy on me," followed by "Lord have mercy on the one who has hurt me." You might imagine a specific hurt as you hold your fists clenched then say aloud, "I let this hurt go" as you open your hands and symbolically release it. Some people find writing a letter to a person who has caused injury and specifically naming or describing the hurt helpful, even if the letter is never sent. (It is usually not wise to send a letter of forgiveness right away. Live with such a letter for a time to make sure the letter is meant for the other person. Often the letter is written for your sake.) Whatever you decide to do, write it down to help you honor this commitment. Place this piece of paper where you will see it on a daily basis.

Write down your plan for the coming week:
This week I will...

Closing Prayer

Pray the following, written by Saint Francis of Assisi, aloud. Should any of the sections be hard for you, offer them as prayers of intention—things you ask God to bring, day by day, into your life.

Lord, make me an instrument of thy peace.
where there is hatred, let me sow love;
where there is injury, pardon;
where there is doubt, faith;
where there is despair, hope;
where there is darkness, light;
and where there is sadness, joy.

O Divine Master,
grant that I may not so much seek
to be consoled as to console;
to be understood, as to understand;
to be loved, as to love;
for it is in giving that we receive,
it is in pardoning that we are pardoned,
and it is in dying that we are born to eternal life.

Lesson Three: Forgiveness as a Process

Scripture: Put away from you all bitterness and wrath and anger and wrangling and slander, together with all malice, and be kind to one another, tenderhearted, forgiving one another, as God in Christ has forgiven you. (Ephesians 4:31-32)

Session Objective: To identify the way accepting forgiveness or offering forgiveness is a process that unfolds over time.

Materials Needed: Pen and paper for written reflections during Personal Reflection Time.

Discussion Questions

1. James Wall suggests that the process of forgiving others begins by first forgiving ourselves. He claims that God deals with us in our innermost parts and speaks these words to us: "You are forgiven, now go and forgive others." Can you describe this experience to someone else?

2. James Wall writes, "The road to forgiveness begins by realizing that we ourselves have acted in ways that others may have

found offensive." How does facing our own potential for hurting others help us forgive others?

3. Can you forgive someone in the absence of regret and an admission of wrongdoing? Does the process of forgiveness have to have a victim, an offender, and a mutual version of the story where one has done wrong and one has been hurt? What happens if you have been harmed by a group or an institution? Is forgiveness possible?

4. Is forgiveness an act of will that is effective even if there is no emotional release or personal reconciliation? Should we focus our minds on forgiveness even when our hearts are not malleable or open?

5. Joseph Coyne has found that painful events that require forgiveness can come to define a person if those event are brooded over long enough to become a part of one's identity. Can you think of persons you know who have allowed past wrongs to define them in some way? What has this done to their capacity for joy or serenity?

6. Confession, we know, is good for the soul. Have you ever confessed your sins to another person, like a clergyperson, or a spiritual friend? How did sharing your guilt or struggle with forgiveness affect you? Are there times when forgiveness requires the help of a third party—someone who will hear your pain and your guilt and represent God for you?

7. Dom Paschal Baumstein says that innocence is required for forgiveness. By innocence he means that we must stand before God and see the truth through God's eyes of goodness. When we are able to see events as God does, forgiveness becomes an act of love. Baumstein says that focusing our forgiveness on God's perspective allows us to boldly say, "I love you; I bear no animosity regarding what passed between us; I do not just tolerate your acts, I embrace you in the love of Christ." Do you believe this type of forgiveness is possible? Have you ever seen it enacted?

8. How do you know when you have been forgiven? What fruits has forgiveness born in your life?

Personal Reflection Time

Read the story of the prodigal son in Luke 15:11-32 and answer the following questions in writing.

1. In what ways are you like the youngest son? Are you estranged from someone you love? Have you squandered some of your time or your resources in ways that you regret?

2. In what ways are you like the father? Whom are you waiting for? Whom do you long to embrace and celebrate his or her return to relationship and intimacy with you? What will you do while you watch and wait and hope?

3. In what ways are you like the older brother? Do you feel someone else has gotten better treatment than you have even when you've worked harder or been more loyal? How does this resentment show in your life? How does it affect your ability to rejoice with others' success and joy?

4. Imagine yourself having to give a welcome home speech at the party for the prodigal. What will you say?

Closing Prayer

Pray the following when you are unable to admit you're wrong:

God,
We want to be forgiving people.
When we are wrong, remind us with your still, small voice.
When others are wrong, give us the grace to let go of the hurt.
When relationships are broken, use us as ambassadors of your mercy.
Help us today and every day to see ourselves and others through your eyes of love. Amen.

Lesson Four: The Repercussions of Forgiveness

Scripture: But you, O Lord, are a God merciful and gracious, slow to anger and abounding in steadfast love and faithfulness. (Psalm 86:15)

Session Objective: To clarify what forgiveness does and does not do in our lives.

Discussion Questions

1. Brendan Walsh describes the "miracle" of South Africa when minority rule was peacefully replaced with democratic majority rule, yet years after the end of apartheid most of the resources still benefit white people and the crime rate is soaring. Are forgiveness and reconciliation possible on a political and social level?

2. When we forgive, we put our desires for retribution or revenge in God's hands. Is letting God mete out punishment enough? What about demanding that things be made right somehow?

3. Where does penitence or making amends fit into forgiveness? Do we have an obligation when we are forgiven to do whatever we can to make things right?

4. Brendan Walsh tells the story of the mother whose son was murdered in South Africa. She said, "It is easy for Mandela and Tutu to forgive.... They lead vindicated lives. In my life nothing, not a single thing, has changed since my son was burned by barbarians.... Therefore I cannot forgive." If nothing at all changes in one's life after forgiving, why should we expect people to go on forgiving?

5. How do we forgive well? How do we remember past hurts or misdeeds without being weighed down by the awfulness of the past? Should we forgive and forget? Is that the real goal? Or are we to forgive so we can once again open ourselves in trust while remembering how trust was betrayed?

6. Brendan Walsh writes, "Seeking and offering forgiveness is an uncomfortable exchange." At one end of the relationship there is shame and embarrassment to face by the one who has done wrong. At the other end there is the reminder that one has been humiliated or abused and treated in an unloving way. To top it off, the one who has been wronged must take the initiative to forgive. If forgiveness is so uncomfortable, why do it at all? Why should we work so hard to forgive if it makes everyone feel so bad before they feel better?

7. Donald Shelby writes, "Forgiveness and love belong together. Indeed, forgiveness makes love possible." Do you agree that it is impossible to love another person without forgiving them?

8. Forgiveness is not passive, not some idle quality that we allow to surface as required. It is an active response. How can you actively pursue forgiveness in your own life and community?

Personal Reflection Time

Donald Shelby defines forgiveness as "a deliberate change of attitude about what has happened....Forgiveness creates, therefore, the possibility for a future together, the opportunity to grow in love and faith together." What would you add or change about this definition from what you have learned from this study? Write your own definition of forgiveness.

(If you are in a group setting, allow time to share your definitions with each other before reciting the closing prayer together.)

Closing Prayer

Make us like you, O God,
merciful and gracious,
slow to anger
and abounding in steadfast love and faithfulness.
We commit ourselves to be forgiving, loving people.
Give us the strength and courage we need to face difficult days.
May we, like Jesus, face those who wrong us with a spirit of
forgiveness.
Help us to say, as Jesus did, "Forgive them, for they know not
what they are doing." Amen.